THE ROYAL COURT THEATRE PRESENTS

Hope has a Happy Meal

by Tom Fowler

Hope has a Happy Meal was first performed at the Royal Court
Jerwood Theatre Upstairs, Sloane Square, on Saturday 3 June 2023.

Hope has a Happy Meal
by Tom Fowler

Cast

Hope **Laura Checkley**
Isla, New Wife + **Mary Malone**
Lor + **Amaka Okafor**
Alex, Angel + **Nima Taleghani**
Clown, Wayne, Ex-husband + **Felix Scott**

Director **Lucy Morrison**
Designer **Naomi Dawson**
Lighting Designer **Anna Watson**
Sound Designer **Annie May Fletcher**
Movement Director **Jonnie Riordan**
Fight Director **Bret Yount**
Assistant Director **Júlia Levai**
Intimacy Consultant **Lucy Hind**

Stage Managers **Caoimhe Regan & Evelin Thomas**

Stage Management Placement **Chloe 'Alex' Alexander**

From the Royal Court, on this production:

Casting Directors **Amy Ball & Arthur Carrington**
Stage Supervisor **Steve Evans**
Lead Producer **Chris James**
Costume Supervisor **Katie Price**
Production Manager **Marius Rønning**
Company Manager **Mica Taylor**

Set built by **Royal Court Stage Department**

Hope has a Happy Meal is a co-production with SISTER.

Tom Fowler (Writer)

For the Royal Court: **Roman Candle** (& Theatre503), **Katzenmusik.**

Other theatre includes: **Suspicious Minds** (Pleasance, Edinburgh Fringe).

Radio includes: **Suspicious Minds.**

Laura Checkley (Hope)

Theatre includes: **Dick Whittington (National); Mother Courage (Southward); Hormonal Housewives (UK tour); Comedy Riot (Leicester Square Theatre); The Wind in the Willows, The Snow Queen (Derby Theatre); Gone with the Wind (New London); By Jeeves (UK tour); Two Cities (Salisbury Playhouse); My Fair Lady (Asia tour); Teechers (Haymarket Theatre Basingstoke & Singapore); House & Garden (Harrogate Theatre); Grease (West End International); Cabaret (English Theatre, Frankfurt); The Boyfriend (UK tour).**

Television includes: **Horseface & Brassic, Screw, Detectorists, In My Skin, King Gary, Porters, Enterprice, Wanderlust, Action Team, Hallmakers, Red Dwarf, This Country, Raised by Wolves, Cradle to the Grave, Coronation Street, Edge of Heaven, W1A, We Are Family, Wasteman, The Agency, The Garden, Criminal Justice, Rosemary & Thyme.**

Film includes: **Whip, Military Wives, Bridget Jones' Baby.**

Naomi Dawson (Designer)

For the Royal Court: **That Is Not Who I Am, Scenes With Girls, The Woods, Men in the Cities** (& Traverse/UK tour).

Other theatre includes: **Akedah, The Breach, The Animal Kingdom, Wildefire, Belongings, The Gods Weep (Hampstead); Fair Play (Bush); Light Falls, Happy Days (Royal Exchange, Manchester); The Convert, The Container, Phaedra's Love, The Pope's Wedding, Forest of Thorns (Young Vic); As You Like It (Regent's Park Open Air); The Duchess of Malfi, Doctor Faustus, The White Devil, The Roaring Girl, As You Like It, King John (RSC); The Winter's Tale (Romateatern, Gotland); The Tin Drum (Kneehigh/Liverpool Everyman/Leeds Playhouse); Beryl (Leeds Playhouse/UK tour); Much Ado About Nothing (Rose, Kingston); Kasimir & Karoline, Fanny & Alexander, Love & Money (Malmö Stadsteater, Sweden); Mirabel (Ovalhouse); Every One (BAC); Weaklings (Warwick Arts Centre); Hotel, Three More Sleepless Nights (National); Brave New World, Dancing at Lughnasa, In Praise of Love (Royal & Derngate, Northampton); Monkey Bars (Unicorn/Traverse); Landscape & Monologue (Ustinov, Bath); Amerika, Krieg der Bilder (Staatstheater Mainz, Germany); Scorched (Old Vic Tunnels); Mary Shelley, The Glass**

Menagerie, Speechless (Shared Experience); The Typist (Sky Arts); King Pelican, Speed Death of the Radiant Child (Drum, Plymouth); If That's All There Is (Lyric, Hammersmith); ...Sisters (& Headlong), State of Emergency, Mariana Pineda (Gate); Stallerhof, Richard III, The Cherry Orchard, Summer Begins (Southwark); Attempts on Her Life, Widows, Touched (BAC); Home, In Blood, Venezuela, Mud, Trash (Arcola).

Opera includes: **Madama Butterfly, The Lottery, The Fairy Queen (Bury Court Opera); Madama Butterfly (Arcola).**

Annie May Fletcher (Sound Designer)

Theatre includes: **Accidental Death of an Anarchist (& West End/Lyric Hammersmith) Rock, (Crucible, Sheffield); Hedwig & the Angry Inch (& HOME Mcr), A Passionate Woman, Decades (Leeds Playhouse); Splintered (Soho); The Odyssey: The Cyclops, Children of the Night (CAST, Doncaster); Brilliant Jerks (Southwark Playhouse); A Christmas Carol, An Adventure (Bolton Octagon); Beauty Queen of Leeanne (Theatre by the Lake); Endurance (Battersea Arts & HOME Mcr); Autopilot (Pleasance, Edinburgh), The Survivor's Guide to Living, Some People Feel the Rain (Manchester Royal Exchange), The Understudy Live (Palace Theatre).**

As associate sound designer, theatre includes: **Carousel (Regent's Park Open Air), Enough (Traverse), How Not To Drown (Glasgow Tron, Lawrence Batley), The Audience (Nuffield Southampton Theatres).**

Digital credits include: **The Entertainment (Summerhall Digital Fringe) 15 Glimpses (Manchester Royal Exchange), Found Fettle (Theatre by the Lake), Oh Woman! (Manchester Royal Exchange), A Passion Play (45North), Luna The Jaguar (Greenpeace UK), Toast, The Understudy (Lawrence Batley).**

Júlia Levai (Assistant Director)

As director, theatre includes: **Smoke (Southwark); We'll Be Who We Are (VAULT); Machinal (St Mary's University); Vanishing, The Prince of Homburg (& Space Arts Centre) (LAMDA); Northern Girls (Pilot); Did I Wake You? (Young Vic); Sweeties (Theatre503); Rage Room (Lyric Hammersmith); The Town (Drayton Arms); There Has Possibly Been An Incident (Blue Elephant/Black Box); Mr Saxon's (The Space/Edinburgh Fringe).**

As assistant director, theatre includes: **All's Well That Ends Well (Royal Shakespeare); L'illusion Comique (National, Belgrade); Nora: A Doll's House (Young Vic); Love Steals Us From Loneliness (LAMDA).**

As associate director, theatre includes: **The Bone Sparrow (UK Tour); Filthy/Rich (Mountview).**

Mary Malone (Isla, New Wife +)

Theatre includes: **As You Like It (Soho Place); The Prince (Southwark); Gulliver's Travels (Unicorn).**

Television includes: **Doctor Who, Vera, Chivalry, The Girlfriend Experience, Play in a Day.**

Radio includes: **Hell Cats 2, Radio Elusia, The Venice Conundrum.**

Awards include: **Winning Graduate (Play in a Day); BroadwayWorld UK Award for Best Supporting Performer in a New Production of a Play (The Prince).**

Lucy Morrison (Director)

For the Royal Court: **Rapture, Scenes with girls, The Woods, MANWATCHING, Plaques & Tangles, Who Cares, Pests, Product (& Clean Break/Traverse/European tour).**

Other theatre includes: **Akedah, The Animal Kingdom (Hampstead); Elephant (Birmingham Rep); Billy the Girl (& Soho), This Wide Night (& Soho), Little on the Inside (& Almeida/Latitude), it felt empty when the heart went at first but it is alright now (& Arcola) (Clean Break); Fatal Light, Doris Day (Soho).**

Lucy is an Associate Director at the Royal Court.

Amaka Okafor (Lor +)

For the Royal Court: **Grimly Handsome, It's All Made Up, The Space Between (The Site), I See You.**

Other theatre includes: **After the End, Glasgow Girls (& National Theatre of Scotland/Citizens) (Stratford East); Nora: A Doll's House (Young Vic); The Son (Kiln/West End); I'm Not Running, Macbeth, Saint George & the Dragon, Peter Pan (National); Hamlet (Barbican/Sonia Friedman & Almeida); Mermaid (Shared Experience); Bird (Root); The Snow Queen (& India tour), Flathampton (Royal & Derngate, Northampton); Beauty & the Beast, The Garbage King, The Tempest, The London Eye Mystery, Cinderella (Unicorn); Dr Korczak's Example (Royal Exchange, Manchester/Arcola); Sabbat (Dukes); Branded, 24 Hour Plays, Hitting Heights (Old Vic); Robin Hood & the Babes in the Wood, Red Oleander, When Brecht Met Stanislavski (Salisbury Playhouse); Meantime (Soho); Tracy Beaker Gets Real (Nottingham Playhouse); Stamping, Shouting & Singing Home (Polka); The Alexander Projekt (Split Moon).**

Television includes: **Bodies, The Responder, Grace, Des, The Split, Vera 10.**

Film includes: **Greatest Days, Sweet Sue.**

Radio includes: **The Unseen Government, No.1 Ladies Detective Agency, Home Front, Dark Fire, Hollywood Ending, If Only, Barnaby Rudge, Time and the Conways, Pilgrim, Dark Side, BBC Radio Drama Company, The Interrogation, Vital Statistics, Mrs Dalloway, The Great Gatsby, The Eggy Doylers, From Fact to Fiction, Marathon Tales.**

Caoimhe Regan
(Stage Manager - Book)

For the Royal Court, as deputy stage manager: **Wish List.**

As stage manager: **The Merchant of Venice (Globe); MUM (FMP/Soho/Royal Theatre Plymouth); Teddy Bears Picnic, A Feast of Bones (& Birmingham Repertory) (Lovett); Sea Change, Ceremony (& Site Specific) (Manchester International Festival); Inside/Outside, Amsterdam, The Double Dealer (Orange Tree); Heart (Kiln); Trad (Livin Dread); Mainstream (Fishamble/Project Arts Centre); CARE, Jockey (WillFredd); After Miss Julie (Prime Cut); Ship of Fools (Draíocht); All Dolled Up: Restitched (THISISPOPBABY/Abbey); Beautiful Dreamers (ANU/Performance Corporation); I HEART ALICE HEART I (HotForTheatre).**

As assistant stage manager: **Into The Woods (Royal Exchange).**

As deputy stage manager, other theatre includes: **Girl From the North Country (UK Tour); 2:22 A Ghost Story (Gielgud); Tao of Glass (& Manchester International Festival), Queen Margaret, Frankenstein, The Suppliant Woman (& Actors Touring Company/Dublin Theatre Festival) (Royal Exchange); An Octoroon (National/Orange Tree); Dummy (MORB/Abbey); The Seagull and Other Birds (PanPan/Noordezon Arts Festival).**

As stage director: **A Christmas Carol (The Gate Dublin).**

As company stage manager: **The 24 Hour Plays (24 Hour Plays Company NYC/Abbey).**

Jonnie Riordan
(Movement Director)

As Director, theatre includes: **Blood Harmony, Eavesdropping (& Traverse), PETRICHOR, AWOL (& Tron), Boy Magnet (& Theatr Clwyd) (ThickSkin); The Witchfinder's Sister (Queen's Theatre Hornchurch); Nigel Slater's Toast (West End/UK Tour).**

As Movement Director, theatre includes: **The Book of Will (& Queen's Theatre Hornchurch/Shakespeare North), A Christmas Carol (Bolton Octagon); How Not to Drown (ThickSkin/Traverse); Great Apes (Arcola); Eyes closed, Ears covered (Bunker); Mobile (The Paper Birds); Home (Frozen Light/UK Tour), Caught (Pleasance), A Tale of Two Cities (USF/Brit Project).**

As Associate Director, theatre includes: **Things I Know to Be True** (Frantic Assembly/UK Tour); **The Static** (& UK Tour), **Blackout, Chalk Farm** (& Bush/Off Broadway) (ThickSkin).

As Associate Movement Director, theatre includes: **Whisper House** (Other Palace), **Myth** (RSC/Mischief Festival).

As assistant stage manager, theatre includes: **First Encounters Twelfth Night** (RSC); **Much Ado About Nothing** (RSC); **The Witchfinder's Sister, Neville's Island** (Queen's, Hornchurch); **As You Like It** (Public Acts Initiative, National); **Two For The Seesaw** (Buckland Theatre Company/West End); **The Book of Will** (Queen's Theatre Hornchurch/Shakespeare North).

Felix Scott
(Clown, Wayne, Ex-husband +)

Theatre includes: **2:22 A Ghost Story** (Criterion); **Dirty Great Love Story** (Arts Theatre); **The Angry Brigade** (Paines Plough); **Gruesome Playground Injuries** (Gate); **The Country Wife** (Manchester Royal Exchange); **The Under Room** (Lyric Hammersmith); **Dr. Faustus** (Globe); **The Maddening Rain** (E.59 Theatre NY/Old Red Lion); **Women Power & Politics** (Tricycle); **Sudden Loss Of Dignity.com** (Bush); **The Man Who Had All The Luck** (Donmar); **In The Heart Of America** (Gielgud); **Sentenced** (Union); **Breakdown** (Pleasance); **Lost Yet Found** (Hampstead); **Nicholas Nickleby, Kes** (Lyric).

Television includes: **Miss Scarlet and The Duke, Our House, The Crown S3, Grantchester, Lee And Dean S2, Ransom, Endeavour S5, No Offence, The Bastard Executioner, The Interceptor, Wolf Hall, Undeniable, Doc Martin, Sirens, Missing, Holby City, The Bill, Plus One, Lewis 11, Wire In The Blood, Victoria Cross Heroes, Sinchronicity, and Bombshell.**

Film includes: **Brothers By Blood, Baghdad In My Shadow, Blitz, Inception, Artifacts.**

Nima Taleghani (Alex, Angel +)

Theatre includes: **Cyrano de Bergerac** (BAM, New York/Playhouse, West End); **Macbeth** (Royal Exchange); **Armadillo** (Yard); **Romeo and Juliet, The Merry Wives of Windsor** (Royal Shakespeare Company); **The Plough and the Stars** (Abbey Theatre) **The White Whale** (Slung Low).

Television includes: **Heartstopper, Danny Boy, Hatton Garden, Casualty.**

Film includes: **Femme, 90 Minutes, Dublin Oldschool.**

Evelin Thomas
(Stage Manager - Props)

For the Royal Court: **NO BORDERS, two Palestinians go dogging.**

As stage manager, theatre includes: **The Flood** (Queen's Hornchurch); **The Great Gatsby Immersive** (Gatsby Mansion, Bond Street); **An Evening with the Good Enough Mum's Club** (Birmingham Hippodrome); **Oklahoma!** (Momentum Performing Arts Academy, Bushey).

Anna Watson (Lighting Designer)

For the Royal Court: **That Is Not Who I Am, Poet in da Corner** (& UK tour), all of it, Pity, You for Me for You, Plaques & Tangles, A Time to Reap.

Other theatre includes: **The Band's Visit, Appropriate, Becoming: Part One, Salt Root & Roe** (Donmar); **All of Us** (National Theatre: Dorfman); **The Bolds,** (Unicorn); **The Winters Tale, Hamlet, Henry VI, Richard III** [as candlelight consultant] (Sam Wanamaker); **Gaslight** (Watford Palace); **The Nut Cracker, Christmas Carol** (Bristol Old Vic); **Leave to Remain, The Seagull, Shopping & Fucking** (Lyric, Hammersmith); **The Fantastic Follies of Mrs Rich, Snow In Midsummer, The Roaring Girl** (RSC); **Twilight: Los Angeles 1992, The Chronicles of Kalki** (Gate); **Box of Delights** (Wilton's Music Hall); **King Lear** (Globe); **Dutchman, The Secret Agent, Fireface, Disco Pigs, Sus** (Young Vic); **Bank on It** (Theatre-Rites/Barbican); **On the Record, it felt empty when the heart went at first but it is alright now** (Arcola); **Paradise, Salt** (Ruhr Triennale, Germany); **Gambling, This Wide Night** (Soho); **Rutherford & Son, Ruby Moon** (Northern Stage); **...Sisters** (Headlong); **King Pelican, Speed Death of the Radiant Child** (Drum, Plymouth).

Dance includes: **Merlin** (Northern Ballet); **Mothers, Soul Play** (The Place); **Refugees of a Septic Heart** (The Garage); **View from the Shore, Animule Dance** (Clore ROH).

Opera includes: **Don Carlo** (Grange Park); **Orlando** (WNO/Scottish Opera/San Francisco); **Cendrillon** (Gyndebourne); **Ruddigore** (Barbican/Opera North/UK Tour); **Critical Mass** (Almeida); **Songs from a Hotel Bedroom, Tongue Tied** (Linbury ROH); **The Bartered Bride** (Royal College of Music); **Against Oblivion** (Toynbee Hall).

Bret Yount (Fight Director)

For the Royal Court: **two Palestinians go dogging, Cyprus Avenue** (& Abbey, Dublin/Public, NYC), **The Cane, Linda, Violence & Son, The Low Road, In Basildon, Wastwater, No Quarter, Belong, Remembrance Day, Redbud, Spur of the Moment, The Nether** (& West End).

Other theatre includes: **The Crucible, Blues for An Alabama Sky, The Middle, Jack Absolute Flies Again, Top Girls, Nine Night, Ma Rainey's Black Bottom, Treasure Island, A Taste of Honey, Emil & the Detectives, The World of Extreme Happiness, Double Feature, Moon on**

a Rainbow Shawl, Men Should Weep (National);
A Little Life, Dirty Dancing, Girl from the North
Country (& Old Vic), City of Angels, Caroline
or Change, Foxfinder, Red Velvet, The Winter's
Tale/Harlequinade, American Buffalo, Bad
Jews, Fences, Posh, Absent Friends, Death
& the Maiden, Clybourne Park, The Harder
They Come, The Lover/The Collection (West
End); Richard III, Private Lives (UK tour);
Waiting for Godot, Romeo & Juliet, The Effect
(Crucible, Sheffield); The Winter's Tale (Cheek
by Jowl); A Very Expensive Poison, The Hairy
Ape (Old Vic); Nine Night, The Wasp (Trafalgar
Studios); The One, Blueberry Toast, First Love
Is the Revolution (Soho); Hamlet (Barbican);
Richard II, The Tempest, Much Ado About
Nothing, Romeo & Juliet, Anne Boleyn (Globe);
Medea (Gate); Tipping the Velvet (Lyric,
Hammersmith); The Pirates of Penzance, La
Traviata, The Mastersingers of Nuremberg, La
Fanciulla, Benvenuto Cellini, Rodelinda (ENO);
King Lear, The Merchant of Venice, Arden of
Faversham, The Roaring Girl, Wolf Hall/Bring
Up the Bodies, Candide (RSC); 'Tis Pity She's
a Whore, The Broken Heart (Sam Wanamaker
Playhouse); Force Majeure, Teenage Dick,
Europe, Appropriate, Splendour, Roots, City of
Angels, The Physicists, The Recruiting Officer
(Donmar); All My Sons, Cannibals, Orpheus
Descending (Royal Exchange, Manchester); The
Trial, A Streetcar Named Desire, A Season in
the Congo, Public Enemy (Young Vic); Ghosts
(& Trafalgar Studios/BAM, NYC), Chimerica
(& West End), Children's Children, The Knot of
the Heart, House of Games, Ruined (Almeida);
The Norman Conquests, A Streetcar Named
Desire, Macbeth, The Caretaker, Lost Monsters
(Liverpool Playhouse/Everyman, Liverpool);
Village Idiots, After the End, Dangerous Lady,
Shalom, Baby, A Clockwork Orange – The
Musical, The Graft, Two Women, Gladiator
Games, Bashment (Theatre Royal, Stratford
East).

Television includes: **Quick Cuts, Against All Odds,
Blue Peter.**

Film includes: **Troy.**

THE ROYAL COURT THEATRE

The Royal Court Theatre is the writers' theatre. It is a leading force in world theatre for cultivating and supporting writers – undiscovered, emerging and established.

Through the writers, the Royal Court is at the forefront of creating restless, alert, provocative theatre about now. We open our doors to the unheard voices and free thinkers that, through their writing, change our way of seeing.

Over 120,000 people visit the Royal Court in Sloane Square, London, each year and many thousands more see our work elsewhere through transfers to the West End and New York, UK and international tours, digital platforms, our residencies across London, and our site-specific work. Through all our work we strive to inspire audiences and influence future writers with radical thinking and provocative discussion.

The Royal Court's extensive development activity encompasses a diverse range of writers and artists and includes an ongoing programme of writers' attachments, readings, workshops and playwriting groups. Twenty years of the International Department's pioneering work around the world means the Royal Court has relationships with writers on every continent.

Since 1956 we have commissioned and produced hundreds of writers, from John Osborne to Jasmine Lee-Jones. Royal Court plays from every decade are now performed on stage and taught in classrooms and universities across the globe.

We strive to create an environment in which differing voices and opinions can co-exist. In current times, it is becoming increasingly difficult for writers to write what they want or need to write without fear, and we will do everything we can to rise above a narrowing of viewpoints.

It is because of this commitment to the writer and our future that we believe there is no more important theatre in the world than the Royal Court.

 royalcourt royalcourttheatre

ROYAL

ASSISTED PERFORMANCES

Captioned Performances

Captioned performances are accessible for people who are D/deaf, deafened & hard of hearing, as well as being suitable for people for whom English is not a first language.

all of it
Friday 16th June 2023, 7:30pm

Hope has a Happy Meal
Wednesday 28th June 2023, 7:45pm
Friday 7th July 2023, 7:45pm

Cuckoo
Wednesday 2nd August 2023, 7:30pm
Thursday 3rd August 2023, 2:30pm
Saturday 12th August 2023, 2:30pm

Word-Play
Wednesday 16th August 2023, 7:45pm
Saturday 26th August 2023, 3pm

BSL-interpreted Performances

BSL-interpreted performances, delivered by an interpreter, give a sign inteprretation of the text spoken and/or sung by artists in the onstage production.

Cuckoo
Saturday 19th August 2023, 2:30pm

ROYAL

ASSISTED PERFORMANCES

Performances in a Relaxed Environment

Relaxed Environment performances are suitable for those who may benefit from a more relaxed environment.

During these performances:
- There is a relaxed attitude to noise in the auditorium; you are welcome to respond to the show in whatever way feels natural
- You can enter and exit the auditorium when needed
- We will help you find the best seats for your experience
- House lights may remain raised slightly
- Loud noises may be reduced

Hope has a Happy Meal
Saturday, 8th July 2023 3pm

Cuckoo
Saturday, 12th July 2023 2:30pm

Word-Play
Saturday, 19th August 2023 3pm

If you would like to talk to us about your access requirements, please contact our Box Office at (0)20 7565 5000 or boxoffice@royalcourttheatre.com

The Royal Court Visual Story is available on our website. Story and Sensory synposes are available on the show pages via the Whats On tab of the website shortly after Press Night.

COURT

ROYAL COURT SUPPORTERS

Our incredible community of supporters makes it possible for us to achieve our mission of nurturing and platforming writers at every stage of their careers. Our supporters are part of our essential fabric – they help to give us the freedom to take bigger and bolder risks in our work, develop and empower new voices, and create world-class theatre that challenges and disrupts the theatre ecology.

To all our supporters, thank you. You help us to write the future.

PUBLIC FUNDING

CHARITABLE PARTNERS

JERWOOD
ARTS

CORPORATE SPONSORS

SIS
TER

Aqua Financial Ltd
Cadogan
Edwardian Hotels, London
Walpole

CORPORATE MEMBERS

Bloomberg Philanthopies
Sloane Stanley

TRUSTS AND FOUNDATIONS

Martin Bowley Charitable Trust
Cockayne – Grants for the Arts
The Noël Coward Foundation
Cowley Charitable Foundation
The D'Oyly Carte Charitable Trust
The Lynne Gagliano Writer's Award
The Golden Bottle Trust
The London Community Foundation
John Lyon's Charity
Clare McIntyre's Bursary
Old Possum's Practical Trust
Richard Radcliffe Charitable Trust
Rose Foundation
John Thaw Foundation
The Victoria Wood Foundation

ROYAL

BAR & KITCHEN

The Royal Court's Bar & Kitchen aims to create a welcoming and inspiring environment with a style and ethos that reflects the work we put on stage. Alongside our vibrant basement bar, you can visit our pop-up outdoor bar Court in the Square.

Offering expertly crafted cocktails alongside an extensive selection of craft gins and beers, wine and soft drinks, our vibrant basement bar provides a sanctuary in the middle of Sloane Square. By day a perfect spot for meetings or quiet reflection and by night atmospheric meeting spaces for cast, crew, audiences and the general public.

All profits go directly to supporting the work of the Royal Court theatre, cultivating and supporting writers - undiscovered, emerging and established.

For more information, visit
royalcourttheatre.com/bar

HIRES & EVENTS

The Royal Court is available to hire for celebrations, rehearsals, meetings, filming, ceremonies and much more. Our two theatre spaces can be hired for conferences and showcases, and the building is a unique venue for bespoke events and receptions.

For more information, visit
royalcourttheatre.com/events

Sloane Square London, SW1W 8AS ⊖ Sloane Square ⇌ Victoria Station
🐦 royalcourt 📘 theroyalcourttheatre 📷 royalcourttheatre

SUPPORT THE COURT AND BE A PART OF OUR FUTURE.

Every penny raised goes directly towards producing bold new writing for our stages, cultivating and supporting new writing in the UK and around the world, and inspiring the next generation of theatre-makers.

You can make a one-off donation by text:

Text **Support 5** to 70560 to donate£5
Text **Support 10** to 70560 to donate £10
Text **Support 20** to 70560 to donate £20

Texts cost the donation amount plus one standard message.
UK networks only.

To find out more about the different ways in which you can get involved, visit our website:

royalcourttheatre.com/support-us

HOPE HAS A HAPPY MEAL

Tom Fowler

Acknowledgments

Writing this play wouldn't have been possible without the guidance, support and patience given in buckets by the following people: Lucy Morrison, Jane Fallowfield, Vicky Featherstone and everyone at the Royal Court Theatre, SISTER, Júlia Levai, Alice Birch, Finn den Hertog, Mark Ravenhill, Iman Qureshi, Chris Sonnex, Mads, Grace Gummer, Gabrielle and Matt Randle-Bent, Max and Naomi Dean, Josh Goulding, Herne Hill Social Club, Peter and Sue, Mum and Dad, Effie and Robin, Flo, Bernie and Zöe Patterson.

T.F.

Characters

HOPE
PASSENGERS
FLIGHT ATTENDANT
WAITRESS/ISLA
NEIGHBOUR
CLOWN
STAGEHANDS
SISTER/LOR
POLICE OFFICER/WAYNE
LORRY DRIVER
FOREST RANGER/ALI
NEW WIFE/PANDORA
EX-HUSBAND/ROY
ANGEL
CUSTOMER

Voice Roles

CAPTAIN
AUDIENCE
TRAIN CONDUCTOR
GROOM
REPORTER
CEO

Multi-Roling

This play should be performed by a minimum of five actors. Voice roles can be distributed however best seen fit. Below is my preference for how characters should be distributed:

Hope

Passenger 1/Stagehand/Forest Ranger/Angel/Customer

Flight Attendant/Neighbour/Sister/Passenger 2

Waitress/Stagehand/New Wife

Clown/Police Officer/Lorry Driver/Ex-Husband

Casting

Hope is a white woman in her mid-forties to mid-fifties.

Lor (Sister) is a Black woman in her mid-forties to mid-fifties.

Isla (Waitress) is a woman in her twenties to early thirties of any ethnicity.

Ali (Forest Ranger) is a man in his late twenties to early thirties of any ethnicity.

Wayne (Police Officer) is a white man in his mid-forties to late fifties.

Isla was assigned male at birth and should never be performed by a cisgender actor. Any other character can be trans/performed by trans actors (excluding Wayne). The pronouns of any character (excluding Wayne) can be changed to they/them if preferred.

This text went to press before the end of rehearsals and so may differ slightly from the play as performed.

1.

HOPE. It's funny, back there in the toilet I was having a little panic attack when I remembered this joke. A joke my mum told me.

It's an old joke so you probably already know it, although – I mean there's so many different versions maybe you don't.

Know this one.

Beat.

It goes –

Once upon a time there's an angel called Norman.

And Norman's not super-senior or anything – you know, he's not an *executive* angel but he does have his own assistants, so –

He's middle management, basically.

Anyway, one day Norman's just sitting in his cloud – just doing his daily sudoku when – *BANG*. He hears this massive crash.

And at first he assumes another angel's caused it –

That maybe Donna in HR has smashed her bonsai tree again except he's looking at Donna and she seems just as confused. In fact, all the angels he can see look confused. And some of them are gasping. Some of them are pointing down from their clouds and actually gasping.

So Norman looks down and ends up gasping too cos what he sees is Earth, the Earth they're meant to be protecting, being invaded by giants – being invaded by massive fucking giants.

Beat.

So this sends the angels into a bit of a panic –

You know, Donna now *does* destroy her bonsai tree –

But Norman stays comparatively calm. He's like, 'Right that is alarming but the execs will know what to do. I may as well have lunch.'

And so he does – he tucks into his lunch. But as he's forking cold risotto into his mouth he gets an e-invite to an urgent angel-wide conference call. So he puts down the fork and joins the call. 'Don't panic,' says the chief exec, 'because we've just sent a message to the giants asking them to leave. So, everything is under control,' she says –

And the rest of the angels clap.

Except it's now five months, twenty conference calls and a hundred and nineteen messages later, and the giants *still* haven't left. You know, Norman's confidence in his superiors is starting to wane.

So one day, today, for the first time ever, Norman raises his hand during a weekly conference call.

'Uh yes, Norman, is it?' says the chief exec.

'Hi, yeah,' says Norman, 'I was just wondering if maybe we need to do more than send messages? Because I've been going through old financial reports and it turns out that for the last fifty years or so we've actually been sort of arming them – sort of mass-selling them the crystals that make our halos shine which gives them their super-strength. And we're *still* supplying it apparently. So, uh – well, what I was thinking is, maybe we should stop that?'

Beat.

'HA HA HA HA HA,' laugh the angels.

'Oh Normycakes,' says the chief exec, 'you are silly, aren't you? But no, I think the sensible course of action would be to send another message and then all wear these T-shirts I've designed that say – "Pick on someone your own size, bitches!" I've got them in purple, yellow and green.'

And then all the angels clap and Norman leaves the call humiliated –

Vowing never to speak in an angel-wide meeting again –

And he doesn't.

Until twenty-four years later, just two months before he's due to retire, Norman gets some troubling news from his doctor.

'Yep – yeah, it's stage-four wing cancer.'

'Oh,' says Norman.

'It's already spread across both of your wings.'

Beat.

'Right.'

Beat.

And this diagnosis –

This sudden wrestling with mortality initially makes Norman very depressed, but eventually gives him a new-found confidence. So much so that during the next angel-wide conference call Norman interrupts, saying –

'Sorry – *sorry*, everyone, but this is bullshit. Because I get that a lot of you are young and new but I've sat in these meetings for twenty-four years now and do you know what our fucking messages have achieved? Nothing, you cunts, absolutely nothing. So listen. Tomorrow morning I'm gonna come into work as normal, I'm gonna have my breakfast, I'm gonna do my sudoku, and then I'm gonna jump off the edge of my cloud and fly down to Earth. And yes, I'm a seventy-four-year-old angel with wing cancer, so alone I'm not much of a threat. But if fifty – forty – even five of you come *with* me, we might actually make a difference somehow. So what do you say, guys? Shall we go and stop some giants?'

Beat.

'HA HA HA HA HA,' laugh the angels.

'Good luck, mate,' says one.

'Yeah I'm sure the giants will be shitting themselves,' says another –

And Norman leaves the call humiliated, again.

But when the next morning comes he thinks, 'You know what, fuck 'em,' and goes to stand at the edge of his cloud.

And he starts to feel quite sick – quite queasy at the thought of taking the plunge because, due to his wing cancer, he's worried he won't be able to fly – that he might just plummet.

Beat.

But then he jumps –

But then he just *jumps* and –

Beat.

Shit.

Pause.

Right, um –

I'm really, really sorry but I've started the wrong joke.

Beat.

Yeah.

See, weirdly my mum had quite a few jokes about giants and, what with the panic attack and the nicotine cravings, I've just got a bit mixed up I think. So, sorry but um – this one –

This one is definitely the one I was thinking about on the toilet –

The one that calmed me down, alright?

It goes like this –

It goes –

Once upon a time there's this washed-up clown called Hope.

And Hope's not a 'clown'-clown – not a red-nose-wearing birthday clown but more of like a storyteller clown. You know, the sort of clown who'll make you laugh *and* cry.

Anyway, one night Hope's finishing a gig at a rural roadside tavern, because this is old-timey, medieval-y times, when –

A seventy-four-year-old angel falls through the roof and kills her.

Beat.

Yeah it's a stupid joke.

But remembering it whilst I was hyperventilating on the toilet calmed me down cos it made me feel like sometimes you just have to jump – just have to try and that's what I'm *doing*, you know? Cos I'm home.

Because I'm finally coming home.

Beat.

So, uh –

Yeah.

Beat.

That's it.

Beat.

*

A moving aeroplane.

Pause.

HOPE. Were you even listening or –

PASSENGER. Yeah I was listening. I've just heard the joke before so –

HOPE. Oh.

    Beat.

    Sorry.

PASSENGER. It's fine.

    Beat.

    You did fuck it up though.

HOPE. What?

PASSENGER. The joke. Cos the clown's name's not Hope, it's *Maurice*.

HOPE. Uh – yeah, no I changed it to my name. You know, to personalise it.

PASSENGER. Well Maurice is objectively funnier.

HOPE. Oh okay.

PASSENGER. Yeah.

HOPE. Cool.

Beat.

Cool.

Pause.

PASSENGER. So can I put my headphones back in now or –

HOPE. What? Oh course, yeah –

PASSENGER. Thanks. (*Puts headphones back in.*)

Announcement chime.

CAPTAIN (*voice-over*). Good evening. This is your captain speaking. Just to say we are *just* about to start our descent into the People's Republic of Koka Kola. Please be advised all passengers will be subjected to a full-cavity search on arrival, and also don't forget to collect your complimentary can of Koke from the customer service desk. On behalf of Koka Kola Airlines I'd like to thank you for joining us and we look forward to seeing you again very, very soon.

Announcement chime.

Beat.

HOPE. Shit.

Beat.

Shit shit shit.

PASSENGER. What are you doing?

HOPE. Panicking.

PASSENGER. What?

HOPE. *Sick*, I'm – I'm gonna be sick.

PASSENGER. Oh god. Right hang on, I'll get out the way.

ATTENDANT. Um, excuse me, madam, but the seatbelt sign's on, see? So I'm going to have to ask you to sit down.

HOPE. Alright –

PASSENGER. No don't sit down – she's about to be sick!

ATTENDANT. Oh. Well, you do have to sit down but – one second, I'll get you a bag.

PASSENGER. For fucksake.

HOPE. I – I don't think I'm able to hold it.

PASSENGER. What? No, you *have* to!

HOPE (*retches*).

PASSENGER. Look, she's got a bag – she's coming! You just have to hold it for three, two, one –

ATTENDANT. Here you go –

HOPE (*vomits into her own hand*).

   Beat.

ATTENDANT. I'll get some cloths.

HOPE (*through hand*). Thank you. Sorry.

   HOPE *stays standing, mouth at hand, vomit slowly leaking through fingers.*

   Behind her, the title of the play appears in bright letters.

   Blackout.

2.

A bar.

HOPE *is on the phone. A beep of an answerphone.*

HOPE. Hi, uh – it's me again. I'm still in the same bar in Skittles Town but I'm assuming you're not coming. So look, can you just call me back please? At least let me know if you're still at the commune, cos – well, cos if you are, I could maybe swing by tomorrow? Because I came here to see you obviously but also it'd be great to have somewhere to stay a couple of nights. So basically yeah, just call me, okay? Bye.

Pause.

WAITRESS. Gin and tonic?

HOPE. Thanks.

Beat.

WAITRESS. Shit, you've not been stood up, have you?

HOPE. What? Oh – uh, *no* – no.

WAITRESS. Phew.

HOPE. Well, sort of actually but by my sister.

WAITRESS. Ah, yeah. I know that game.

HOPE. Do you?

WAITRESS. Yeah. Although with us it was usually me standing *her* up.

HOPE. I mean same here really but… it's alright, she said she'd meet me tomorrow instead. She co-runs a commune so she's pretty busy.

WAITRESS. Cool. Well, that's last orders on the bar so –

HOPE. Oh, one second. (*Starts downing her drink.*)

WAITRESS. Whoa – no I wasn't asking you to down it, I was just saying –

HOPE (*finishes*). No, it's so I can order another.

WAITRESS. Oh, right. Gin and tonic?

HOPE. Thanks.

WAITRESS. I'll grab it now.

Beat.

HOPE. Hey, you don't know anywhere still open, do you? Like, after this?

WAITRESS. I uh – I do actually. I was thinking of going after I finish.

HOPE. Oh.

Beat.

Do you think I could maybe –

*

A club.

Loud house music.

HOPE *and* WAITRESS *dancing.*

HOPE. COME ON! DON'T YOU THINK IT'S WEIRD?

WAITRESS. NO, I *DO* THINK IT'S WEIRD –

HOPE. BECAUSE BEFORE – BEFORE YOU WERE BORN, THIS WAS LIKE A PROPER DEMOCRATIC COUNTRY WITH PROPER PLACE NAMES AND STUFF.

WAITRESS. WAS IT?

HOPE. YEAH.

WAITRESS. BUT WAS IT?

HOPE. YEAH.

WAITRESS. NO BUT WAS IT REALLY THOUGH?

HOPE. WHAT?

WAITRESS. I SAID, WAS IT *REALLY*?

HOPE. *OH*.

WAITRESS. BECAUSE YEAH YOU HAD ELECTIONS, BUT WASN'T IT STILL JUST ABOUT MONEY? JUST ABOUT WHO BEST REPRESENTED THE INTERESTS OF CAPITAL?

HOPE. TRUE, YEAH.

WAITRESS. WHAT?

HOPE. *TRUE.*

Pause.

CIG?

*

A smoking area.

WAITRESS (*showing* HOPE *photo on phone*). That's my boy there.

HOPE. Your son?

WAITRESS. Well, my nephew but um…

HOPE. What?

WAITRESS. Never mind actually.

HOPE. What is it?

WAITRESS. No, it's just not a fun topic of conversation.

HOPE. Well, that's okay.

WAITRESS. No, s'alright. We'll save it.

HOPE. Sure?

WAITRESS. Yeah.

Beat.

Anyway. You'll get to meet him now.

HOPE. What?

WAITRESS. Well, I'm assuming you're crashing, right? With me.

HOPE. Oh. Um, if that's okay?

WAITRESS. Course. My neighbour looks after him – you know, when I work nights. But we're already gonna be way later than I said I'd be, so we should go now cos she'll be pissed.

HOPE. Alright, but can we eat something first please?

WAITRESS. Yeah? What're you thinking?

Beat.

HOPE. Um…

*

A pavement.

Both sat on floor.

WAITRESS *eating McDonald's.*

HOPE *staring up at sky.*

Pause.

WAITRESS. You've barely touched yours.

HOPE. Oh, I'm uh – not that hungry in the end.

WAITRESS. Mm, yeah that'll be the shrooms.

HOPE. Probably.

WAITRESS. Definitely.

HOPE. Hey, you don't believe anything's up there, do you?

WAITRESS. *Up* there?

HOPE. Yeah.

WAITRESS. Like what?

HOPE. Like – I don't know. Like not gods but like angels – like monsters.

WAITRESS. Nah. I think all that's down here.

HOPE. Do you?

WAITRESS. Yeah. No, I think if there's anything like that then they're among us, you know? Like, *we're* the angels, *we're* the monsters.

HOPE. So what does that make me?

WAITRESS. An angel, love.

HOPE. Nice.

WAITRESS. And I'm an angel too, obviously.

HOPE. And so then who are the monsters?

WAITRESS. I mean I'm not gonna write you a fucking list, mate.

HOPE. Fair.

WAITRESS. You can just tell.

Beat.

My sister was an angel.

HOPE. Yeah?

WAITRESS. Yeah.

Beat.

WAITRESS *sees the time*.

Oh shit, we should go.

HOPE. Okay.

WAITRESS. You really not gonna eat that?

HOPE. Nah.

WAITRESS. Well, bring it for Mrs R then. Might sugar the pill a bit.

HOPE. But surely she won't be up?

WAITRESS. No she'll definitely be up, she barely sleeps.

HOPE. Are you really that scared of her?

WAITRESS. Yeah! I mean she's a fucking sweetheart, but she can be quite –

HOPE. What?

WAITRESS. Quite –

*

A living room.

NEIGHBOUR *holds sleeping baby.*

All whisper not to wake it.

NEIGHBOUR. Cold McDonald's!? Cold McDonald's!?

WAITRESS. *Sorry!*

NEIGHBOUR. What am I gonna do with cold McDonald's?

WAITRESS. I –

NEIGHBOUR. Eat it like some kind of *animal*?

WAITRESS. No, I – well, *maybe*, I –

NEIGHBOUR. *No*. No I *never* want cold McDonald's! All I want is –

WAITRESS. For me to call you if I'm running late.

NEIGHBOUR. Yes! And is that too much to ask?

WAITRESS. No –

NEIGHBOUR. No it's not, no.

WAITRESS. No.

HOPE (*not whispering*). Although, in her defence –

WAITRESS. Shh –

NEIGHBOUR. *Shush*. The *baby*, woman.

HOPE. Sorry.

Beat.

NEIGHBOUR. Listen. You know I don't mind watching the baby –

WAITRESS. I know –

NEIGHBOUR. I *love* the baby. And if you need me to stay an extra couple of hours so you can go out and have fun with *this* weird woman, that's fine too. But what is absolutely *not* fine is –

WAITRESS. Me not calling.

NEIGHBOUR. Thank you.

WAITRESS. No, it won't happen again.

NEIGHBOUR. Well, let's leave it at that then. (*To baby.*) Goodbye, my little munchkin. Mwah-mwah-mwah-mwah-*mwah*.

Hands baby to WAITRESS.

WAITRESS. Thanks so much, Mrs R.

NEIGHBOUR. Pleasure. And um next week it's Tuesday, Thursday, *Saturday*?

WAITRESS. Yeah. And I promise not to bring you McDonald's.

NEIGHBOUR. No – no, I said no *cold* McDonald's. Warm McDonald's is fine – I'd have it.

WAITRESS. Okay.

NEIGHBOUR. Well, goodbye now –

WAITRESS. Bye –

HOPE. Bye –

Beat.

HOPE *and* WAITRESS *launch into giggles.*

Once they stop giggling, WAITRESS *holds baby in silence.*

HOPE *watches.*

WAITRESS. Um, do you want to hold him?

HOPE. Oh, uh –

WAITRESS. You don't have to –

HOPE. No, I uh – want to, I was just uh – Yeah.

WAITRESS. Yeah?

HOPE. Yeah.

WAITRESS. Alright, well *this* then – (*Passing baby.*) is Isaac. Oh and I'm Isla, by the way. I just realised we never did that.

HOPE. Oh yeah. Um, I'm Hope.

Pause.

WAITRESS. He's beautiful, isn't he?

HOPE. Yeah.

Beat.

WAITRESS. Right, I'm just gonna go sort your bed out.

HOPE. I mean I'd be fine on the sofa.

WAITRESS. Yeah you're *on* the sofa.

HOPE. Oh.

WAITRESS. I just meant I'm gonna get your duvet and a sheet and stuff.

HOPE. Okay, yeah.

WAITRESS. So will you be alright with him for a few minutes?

HOPE. What? Oh, uh *yeah*, yeah cos – I mean you're not gonna be long, are you?

WAITRESS. What?

HOPE. I just mean, um –

WAITRESS. No. No, I'm literally just getting some stuff out a cupboard and brushing my teeth and that. But I uh – can take him *with* me, if you're –

HOPE. No – no, that should be fine.

WAITRESS. Right, two ticks then.

WAITRESS *leaves.*

HOPE *holds baby, increasingly tense and uncomfortable.*

Sound of giant's footsteps.

HOPE. Hel*lo*?

Beat.

Game-show theme tune plays.

*

A game show.

CLOWN. Gooooood evening! My name is – (*Unintelligible.*) and you're watching…

AUDIENCE (*chanting*). WHO'S, THE, WORST, PER, SON, IN, THE, *WORLD*!

STAGEHANDS *rush in, take baby from* HOPE*, touch up her hair and make-up, and exit.*

CLOWN. Our first contestant is back in the country after a twenty-four-year 'spiritual journey', let's give a big warm welcome *to…* Hope!

AUDIENCE (*applauds*).

CLOWN. So how are you feeling, Hope? Ready to see if you're the worst person in the world?

HOPE. Where am I?

CLOWN. Ooh, well, *that* doesn't bode well!

AUDIENCE (*laughs*).

CLOWN. Now, as always, we'll start with the our super-quick 'What's the Beef?' round. And the rules are very simple. *I'm* going to read out names of people who hate you and *you*, Hope, will tell me why. Got it?

HOPE. I think so but –

CLOWN. So, are we ready, folks?

AUDIENCE. YES!

CLOWN. We'll put thirty seconds on the clock and your time starts…

Beat.

Now – Michael MacFarlane.

HOPE. Who?

CLOWN. Michael MacFarlane. If you don't know, pass.

HOPE. Um, pass.

CLOWN. Annika Erikson.

HOPE. Oh, um – because I broke up with her?

CLOWN. No because you slept with her brother *then* broke up with her.

AUDIENCE (*laughs*).

CLOWN. Diego Santos.

HOPE. Because I left him at the altar?

CLOWN. Nope. The clock's *ticking*, Hope. Katrin Wolff.

HOPE. Pass.

CLOWN. Sam Cote.

HOPE. Pass.

CLOWN. Steve Lee.

HOPE. Pass.

CLOWN. Sylvia Seagrave – your own *mother*.

   Beat.

HOPE. I…

   Theme tune.

CLOWN. Well, that's the end of that round and all I can say is… ouch.

AUDIENCE (*laughs*).

CLOWN. No correct answers so we move to Round *Two*…

AUDIENCE (*chanting*). DO YOU, REALLY, KNOW, WHAT THEY *THINK*, OF, YOU?

CLOWN. And for this round we're gonna welcome onto the stage our very special guest… that's right, it's Hope's sister, Lor Seagrave.

AUDIENCE (*cheers and applause*).

HOPE. Lor?

CLOWN. No conferring please. Now before we begin, tell us… until now when was the last time you *saw* Hope?

SISTER. It was twenty-four years ago when she left the country.

CLOWN. She never visited?

SISTER. No.

CLOWN. Never called?

SISTER. Nothing.

CLOWN. Not even a Christmas card? Now that's *cold*!

AUDIENCE (*laughs*).

HOPE. But wait cos I've been *calling*! Since arriving I've been calling but –

CLOWN. Shut the fuck up. So, Lor, backstage you were asked to write ten words – a mixture of positive *and* negative words that you would use to describe your sister. So, Hope, all you have to do is correctly guess three of those words. Are we ready?

AUDIENCE. YES!

CLOWN. Then your first word please, Hope?

HOPE. Um… selfish?

Bing.

CLOWN. Correct!

AUDIENCE (*applause*).

CLOWN. And now your *second* word, please.

HOPE. Maybe… flighty?

Bing.

CLOWN. Correct!

AUDIENCE (*applause*).

CLOWN. Wow, maybe you're *not* the worst person in the world! Just one more correct answer and you're free. So one last word please, Hope?

Beat.

HOPE. Loving?

Beat.

Buzzer.

CLOWN. Nope, that's a wrong answer I'm afraid! Lor does *not* think you're loving, do you, Lor?

SISTER. Not at all, no.

CLOWN. In fact, Lor didn't use *any* positive words to describe you.

AUDIENCE (*laughs*).

CLOWN. Which means we move to the final round…

AUDIENCE. SPOT, YOUR, *SON*!

HOPE. What?

CLOWN. And this is the round where we find out if Hope really *is* the worst person in the world. But, before we start, we'll need to bring out the…

AUDIENCE (*chanting*). WHEEL, OF, PUNISHMENT!

CLOWN. That's right. Because if Hope *is* the worst, we can't let her walk away unscathed, can we?

AUDIENCE. NO!

CLOWN. *No.*

> STAGEHANDS *bring on the wheel. Options include electric chair, life imprisonment, waterboarding, starvation, flaying, bury alive and fingernails.*
>
> So… what will Hope's punishment be? Would you do us the honour and spin the wheel, Lor?

SISTER. Now?

CLOWN. Please.

> SISTER *spins wheel.*
>
> *Drum roll.*
>
> And if Hope fails the next round her punishment will *be…*
>
> *Drum roll stops.*
>
> *Beat.*
>
> Waterboarding!

AUDIENCE (*cheers*).

CLOWN. She will be waterboarded.

HOPE. Wait, no –

CLOWN. Calm down, Hope, we're not there yet! Although actually, can we get her pinned down now? Just so we're ready and –

STAGEHANDS *enter and approach* HOPE.

Thank you.

HOPE. Stop. What are you doing? Stop. *Stop!*

STAGEHANDS *pin* HOPE *down to sofa and cover her mouth.*

HOPE*'s shouts become muffled.*

Another enters with a large bucket of water, a cloth, and a glass.

CLOWN. Because when Hope left the country twenty-four years ago, she didn't *just* abandon her sister and mother. No, she *also* abandoned… her son!

AUDIENCE (*gasps*).

CLOWN. I know. And he was only a baby!

AUDIENCE (*boo*).

One audience member shouts 'cunt!'

CLOWN (*laughs*). Hold your horses. Hope still has a chance to redeem herself. See, in a second, we're gonna show three photographs of young men and one of them will be Hope's son, Mitch. All she has to do is spot him.

AUDIENCE (*applause*).

CLOWN. So, Hope.

STAGEHANDS *present three photographs of young men.*

Which one's your son?

STAGEHANDS *remove hand from* HOPE*'s mouth.*

Pause.

HOPE. I –

CLOWN. Chop-chop, Hope. I'm gonna need an answer.

HOPE. I – don't *know*.

CLOWN. Let's give her a countdown, shall we?

HOPE. Wait, I –

AUDIENCE. FIVE –

HOPE. I need more time, I –

AUDIENCE. FOUR –

HOPE. Stop –

AUDIENCE. THREE –

HOPE. Please –

AUDIENCE. TWO –

HOPE. *STOP* –

AUDIENCE. *ONE…*

HOPE. I – the one on the left then, he's my son.

> *Beat.*

> *Buzzer.*

CLOWN. Wrong answer!

> STAGEHANDS *cover* HOPE*'s mouth again.*

> *Muffled screams.*

> *They place cloth on her face.*

> *A* STAGEHAND *scoops water from bucket with glass.*

> *They begin to waterboard* HOPE.

*

Darkness.

Sound of waterboarding.

CLOWN. Any last words, Hope?

Sound of HOPE *drowning, trying to resist.*

I can't hear you!

AUDIENCE (*laughs*).

CLOWN. Hope.

Beat.

Hope.

                                       *

Living room (with lights off).

HOPE *asleep on sofa.*

ISLA *throws glass of water over* HOPE*'s face.*

ISLA (*whispering*). *Hope!*

HOPE (*gasps*).

ISLA (*finger at mouth*). Shh.

   Banging on door.

OFFICER (*voice*). OI! I know you're fucking *in* there, Isla!

HOPE (*whispering*). What's happening?

ISLA (*whispering*). We need to go. Like, *now* – out the window.

HOPE (*whispering*). What?

OFFICER (*voice, banging on door*). Open the fucking door, you bitch!

ISLA (*whispering*). Look, I'll explain once we're out but we've got to go, okay?

HOPE (*whispering*). Okay.

ISLA (*whispering*). I'll grab Isaac.

   ISLA *leaves.*

   HOPE *sits up.*

   Banging on door continues.

OFFICER (*voice*). He's my fucking son, Isla!

Banging.

Isla.

Banging.

ISLA!

Blackout.

3.

A toilet on a moving train.

HOPE *and* ISLA *stand opposite each other.*

ISLA *holds baby.*

Announcement chime.

CONDUCTOR (*voice-over*). Good morning, my beautiful little cherubs, and welcome aboard the Koka Kola Railway service to Nike International. Today's train calls at Walmart Market, Volkswagen Junction, Disney Quarry, Samsung Central, Mitsubishi Parkway and Nike International. Please remember to take all rubbish and luggage with you when departing the train. Thanks, and enjoy the rest of your journey.

Announcement chime.

Pause.

ISLA. Quite cosy, isn't it?

HOPE. Yeah.

Beat.

Sorry, *why* are we in here again?

ISLA. Weren't you listening?

HOPE. I *was* listening but –

ISLA. He's a fucking police officer, Hope.

HOPE. Yeah I know all that but why can't we sit out *there*?

ISLA. Cos out there there's cameras and shit.

HOPE. But surely he can't see them – can't have access to them, can he?

ISLA. I mean I don't know what he has but he somehow did manage to find me so, if it's alright with you, I'd like to be a little bit cautious.

HOPE. Yeah fine but… I dunno, it just doesn't make sense to me.

ISLA. *What* doesn't?

HOPE. Well if, like you say, he *did* kill your sister then –

ISLA. Wait, what do you mean, 'if'?

HOPE. I just mean –

ISLA. Do you not believe me?

HOPE. I – No I *do*, I just find it hard to believe nothing would've happened to him, you know? That he'd get away with it – get to keep his job.

ISLA. Oh *do* you?

HOPE. Yeah.

ISLA. Then where the fuck have you been, Hope? What fucking country have *you* been living in?

HOPE. What, *recently* or –

ISLA. *Any* time.

HOPE. I mean I was here – I was born here and then I left when I was twenty, before it became the Republic, and since I've lived in Microsoftia, Teslazuela, the United States of Nescafé – all over really.

ISLA. And in all those places the police were held accountable, were they?

HOPE. Well –

ISLA. Police officers were never let off after 'accidentally' killing the wrong woman, Black person, queer person, migrant, activist –

HOPE. I –

ISLA. Because I don't believe that for a fucking second. But hey, if you trust them over me – if you believe them that my sister took her own life two days after *leaving* that abusive, evil cunt – then fine, you do you. But you can fuck off out that door please cos I don't want anything to do with you.

ISLA presses the 'open door' button and the door opens.

She sits on the toilet.

Pause.

PASSENGER 2 (*appears in doorway*). Um, are you done in here or –

HOPE (*pressing 'close door' button*). No!

PASSENGER 2 (*leaves, flustered*).

The door closes.

HOPE *and* ISLA *smile at each other.*

Beat.

HOPE. Sorry.

ISLA. It's okay.

HOPE. You're right, I guess I haven't been paying attention.

ISLA (*nods*).

HOPE. So, um – what now?

ISLA (*shrugs*). I mean last time he found me I travelled across half the country and then started again so, I guess maybe *that*?

HOPE. Well, I was meant to visit my sister's commune today. How about you hide out there? You know, at least for a bit anyway.

ISLA. You sure she wouldn't mind?

HOPE. Definitely.

ISLA. Okay.

HOPE. It's in what's now the BP Nature Reserve so we can get off at Disney Quarry and walk. But like you say, *until* then we should stay in here.

ISLA. Cool.

Beat.

I do actually need a wee though.

HOPE. Me too.

ISLA. If we take turns holding the baby then –

HOPE. Yeah let's do that.

ISLA. Here, you can go first.

HOPE. You sure?

ISLA. Yeah hold on… (*Stands and hugs wall so* HOPE *can pass*.)

HOPE *passes*.

There.

HOPE *lifts seat and sits down*.

ISLA, *holding baby, turns to face wall*.

HOPE *starts weeing*.

Announcement chime.

CONDUCTOR (*voice-over*). Sorry to bother you delightful sugar plums again but this is just a quick security announcement to say that if you happen to see a young woman, an older woman and a baby travelling together, please alert a member of staff immediately.

ISLA. Shit.

CONDUCTOR (*voice-over*). Otherwise our next scheduled stop will be Walmart Market in approximately six minutes.

Announcement chime.

ISLA. Um –

HOPE. What do we do?

ISLA. Well, are you finished?

HOPE. Almost.

ISLA. Right you finish up, *I'll* go, and then we'll get off here.

HOPE. And walk?

ISLA. Yeah?

HOPE. That'll take *days*.

ISLA. I –

Knocking on door.

HOPE *quietly pulls pants and trousers up and stands*.

Beat.

Knocking.

PASSENGER 2 (*off*). Hey. Look, I'm not gonna report you, just let me in.

ISLA looks at HOPE *as if asking, 'Should we?'*

HOPE *shrugs*.

Beat.

ISLA *presses the 'open door' button and the door opens.*

PASSENGER 2 *enters quickly.*

ISLA *presses the 'close door' button and it closes.*

Right hello, I'm Sharon, and I'm a nurse.

HOPE *and* ISLA. Hi Sharon.

PASSENGER 2. Now where're you trying to get to?

HOPE. The BP Nature Reserve?

PASSENGER 2. Then this is what you do – you're gonna get off here, you're gonna walk out the station and then through the shopping centre as quickly as you can. And then, once you're in the car park, you're gonna call this number.

Hands ISLA *a napkin with writing on.*

Now he will probably sound grumpy but all you need to say is it's urgent, that Sharon sent you, and that you're already in Location D. Then after, whenever he arrives, he'll drive you as far as he can. Any questions?

HOPE. Um –

PASSENGER 2. Oh and I almost forgot. He won't charge you but he *will* be expecting lunch so if you can grab him a Maccies whilst you're waiting, that'll be fine. Just a large Big Mac meal with a McFlurry. You got cash?

ISLA. Yeah –

HOPE. Yeah.

PASSENGER 2. I'll stand outside till we stop.

Presses 'open door' button.

Door opens.

ISLA. Wait, why are you helping us?

PASSENGER 2 *presses 'close door' button and leaves.*

Door closes.

Beat.

HOPE. I uh – guess we just do *that* then.

ISLA. Yeah.

HOPE *flushes toilet.*

Pause.

HOPE. Did you still need a wee or –

ISLA. Oh yeah.

Blackout.

*

A moving lorry.

LORRY DRIVER *wears an eyepatch and drinks from a McDonald's cup.*

'I Saw the Light' by Hank Williams is playing in the lorry.

HOPE. So uh – how do you know Sharon?

LORRY DRIVER. Huh? (*Turns down music.*)

HOPE. I said how do you know *Sharon*? You know, the –

LORRY DRIVER. Through AA.

HOPE. Oh.

LORRY DRIVER. She runs a group out in Nike City. I've been going for nine years now.

HOPE. Have you?

LORRY DRIVER. Almost. You know, not that I've been clean all that time – like there has been lapses but whenever I *have* tripped up she's been there, you know? So, when she asked if I'd do this – join her sort-of network, I said yes. Cos I mean I'm doing these routes anyway – you know, transporting all these *biscuits* back and forth so I thought why *not* help out? And it's kind of amazing, this secret-network thing cos apparently there's hundreds of us now, all across the country. And it's not just drivers and nurses – there's also lawyers, brickies, teachers, shopkeepers – allsorts. All doing their bit to help whoever needs it most – whoever the big boys are trampling on. And that's why I love this *song* so much, you know? This kind of music.

HOPE. What, Christian music?

LORRY DRIVER. Yeah. Cos I'm not Christian or anything – you know, I don't believe in God but all the stuff about darkness – about being in darkness and finding the light, it speaks to me cos that's what *happened*, you know? Like, not that long ago I was barely holding a job down, spewing my guts at my daughter's oboe recital but now I'm sober, my daughter's speaking to me again and also I'm *part* of something, you know? Part of something doing good.

Beat.

Anyway.

Beat.

Thanks again for the McDonald's.

HOPE. It's alright.

LORRY DRIVER. I should've said but I can only take you as far as Facebook Forest cos then my route goes *west* there, if that's okay?

HOPE. Course, yeah.

LORRY DRIVER (*nods*).

Song ends.

Pause.

Um, do you mind if I play it again?

HOPE. What? Oh, uh – no.

LORRY DRIVER. Thanks.

Song starts to play again.

Blackout.

*

Darkness.

RANGER (*off*). Help! Help, I changed my mind!

HOPE (*off, in distance*). Hello?

RANGER (*off*). Help, I'm slipping! Help!

HOPE (*off*). Oh my god –

ISLA (*off*). Um – right *quickly*, let me get on your shoulders.

HOPE (*off*). Oh, uh –

ISLA (*off*). No, left a bit – left a bit…

> *Beat.*

> There.

*

A chopped-down forest.

FOREST RANGER, *hanging from the lone standing tree by a noose around his neck, is sitting on* ISLA *who is sat on* HOPE*'s shoulders. The baby is on the floor.*

RANGER (*gasps*). Jesus fucking Christ.

HOPE. Are you okay?

RANGER. No. No, I mean I'm not dead which is something so thank you but I probably wouldn't say I'm okay, no.

> *Pause.*

ISLA. Are you going to take the noose off then or –

RANGER. Oh, yeah. (*Tries to take noose off.*)

> *Beat.*

ISLA. Have you got it?

RANGER. No, I – I can't do it.

ISLA. What?

RANGER. I can't get it off, it's too tight.

ISLA. Fucksake.

RANGER. I do have a knife but it's in my bag.

HOPE. Which is where?

RANGER. *There*.

> HOPE *and* ISLA *turn to see a bag on the floor, way out of reach*.

HOPE. Yeah fuck that.

ISLA. Right, lower your head as far as you can.

RANGER. What?

ISLA. Lower your head, I'm gonna yank it off.

RANGER. Wait no –

> ISLA *pulls* FOREST RANGER *towards her and starts trying to pull the noose off*.

Ow – you're hurting me!

> HOPE *starts to lose balance*.

HOPE. Careful.

> *They all wobble*.

> *Careful –*

> ISLA *yanks the noose off and they all topple to the ground*.

> HOPE *and* ISLA *sit up and sigh in relief*.

RANGER. What the hell? (*Standing up*.) You fucking – fucking maniac!

ISLA. Excuse me?

RANGER. You heard me! You've given me fucking rope burn.

ISLA. Um, I've just saved your life, you shit.

RANGER. I…

> *Beat*.

> *I…*

> *Beat*.

Baby starts to cry.

ISLA *goes to him, picks him up and cradles him.*

ISLA. Hey it's okay, Isaac. Mummy's here. Mummy's here.

Baby stops crying.

She walks back and sits with HOPE.

FOREST RANGER *stands dazed then eventually sits too.*

Pause.

HOPE. So, um – what's your name?

RANGER. Huh? Oh, it's um – Ali.

HOPE. Hi, Ali. I'm Hope.

ISLA. I'm Isla.

HOPE. And the baby's Isaac.

RANGER (*nods*).

HOPE. You got any food in that bag, Ali?

RANGER. No.

HOPE. Oh.

RANGER. There might be stuff in the cabin but I didn't think I'd need to eat again. Like, ever, so…

Beat.

HOPE. Here.

RANGER. What?

HOPE. Come here.

FOREST RANGER *sidles towards* HOPE.

HOPE *puts her arm around him. He is uneasy at first but relaxes into it. Eventually, with gentle coaxing, he rests his head on her shoulder.*

ISLA *continues to gently rock baby.*

'I Saw the Light' by Hank Williams plays.

Blackout.

*

Darkness.

A small fire crackles into life.

*

A small log cabin with a wood burner.

HOPE *drinks from a label-less bottle of clear booze.*

HOPE. So wait – you actually live in here?

ALI. Yeah. I mean the cabin comes with the job.

HOPE. Oh.

ALI. So it's not mine, it's for whoever's the forest ranger.

HOPE. Right.

ALI. Except now there's no forest and as of tomorrow no forest *ranger*, so it's gonna be a mess room apparently. You know, for the builders building the flats. (*Shrugs.*) Oh well. I did try.

HOPE *offers bottle.*

ALI *takes it and swigs.*

ISLA. So um – what're you gonna do now?

ALI. Fuck knows. Like, for eight years trying to look after the forest has been my whole life, you know? And I mean I did have a plan but then in the last minute I realised it was a fucking stupid, *pointless* plan, which you thankfully stopped. So now I'm planless.

ISLA. Well, you can come with us, if you want.

ALI. Really?

ISLA. Yeah.

ALI. Where're you going?

ISLA. To her sister's commune.

ALI. Oh.

ISLA. Tell him what it's like, Hope – about the vegetables and stuff.

HOPE. I mean I haven't been in a very long time but uh – yeah, it's amazing. You know, there's about eighty, ninety people living in what was once my nan's farm and they grow their own food, they generate their own green power, it's beautiful.

ALI. Wow.

ISLA. And I mean I'm not sure how long we'll be staying but at least a while.

ALI. Yeah, no – that sounds great.

ISLA. Yeah?

ALI. Yeah.

ISLA. Great. Um, will be that okay, Hope? With your sister?

HOPE. Uh – yeah, definitely.

ISLA. You wanna check?

Beat.

HOPE. Now?

ISLA (*shrugs*).

HOPE. Fine. I'll uh – go call her now.

ISLA. Thank you.

HOPE *leaves.*

Beat.

ALI. I might go too actually. For a piss.

ISLA. Oh.

ALI. If that's alright?

ISLA. Course, yeah.

ALI. That's something I'm looking forward to actually. Having a proper toilet.

ISLA. Right. Although I don't know if there is one in the commune, to be fair.

ALI. Ah.

ISLA. I mean you'd assume so but you never know, do you?

ALI. True. Either way, at least I'm able to piss. Thanks to you. You know, cos I'm not – um –

ISLA. Dead?

ALI. Yeah.

Beat.

That sounded a lot smoother in my head.

ISLA. Did it?

ALI. Yeah I guess I just mean thank you. Genuinely. You seem great.

Beat.

Anyway, um –

ISLA. Yep –

ALI. I'm just gonna – one second –

ISLA. Cool.

ALI *leaves*.

ISLA *smiles*.

She starts to rock baby gently.

So… what do you think of Ali, Isaac? He's cute, isn't he? He is – he *is* cute. Yeah he's obviously damaged but who isn't? Your mum's damaged, your other mum was damaged, you will *definitely* be damaged… that's just the way it is. I know. I know, it's *not* fair but what you gonna do?

Knock on door.

How was the piss?

She turns to face door.

POLICE OFFICER *enters pointing gun at* ISLA.

Beat.

OFFICER. What? You thought you could run forever?

Beat.

The *baby*, Isla. Give me my baby.

Beat.

NOW.

ISLA. No.

OFFICER. *What?*

ISLA. I said no, Wayne – *please*, just – just –

OFFICER. Just what? Just fucking let you raise my boy? Without me? Without his dad? No, no a boy *needs* his dad and – and well, that's what I was trying to tell your sister when –

ISLA. When what?

OFFICER. When –

ISLA. When you killed her?

OFFICER. I – I – I didn't mean to, alright? I was trying – I was just trying to –

ISLA. What?

OFFICER. To explain. To make her see that leaving me, leaving Isaac without his mum *and* dad – without that stability was wrong – was selfish. But she wouldn't listen – she refused to just *listen* –

ISLA. And so you –

OFFICER. Stop! Look, I get that you care about him but whatever you fucking tell yourself you're never gonna be his mum, alright? So be fucking sensible now and give me my boy.

Beat.

ISLA *reluctantly but gently passes the baby to* POLICE OFFICER.

He takes it gently.

Thank you.

Beat.

One day I might let you see him again. One day, maybe, when he's older and you've calmed down a bit. But until then, if I ever see you without having contacted you, I will kill you. Understood?

Beat.

Understood?

ISLA (*nods*).

OFFICER. Good. (*Goes to leave.*)

ISLA. *Wait.*

Beat.

Can I at least say goodbye?

OFFICER. No.

ISLA. I won't come after you or anything – I'll leave you alone, I just wanna say goodbye to him.

Beat.

Please?

OFFICER (*hesitates*). Fine.

ISLA. Thank you.

OFFICER. *Quickly* though.

ISLA (*approaches*). Goodbye, Isaac. Bye. Goodbye, good–

> ALI *rushes in and stabs* POLICE OFFICER *in the back of his shoulder.*

> POLICE OFFICER *cries out and drops his gun.*

OFFICER. FUCKER.

> ISLA *takes the baby.*

> ALI *takes the gun and gets* POLICE OFFICER *to his knees.*

ALI. Here, the gun.

> ISLA *takes the gun from* ALI *and points it at* POLICE OFFICER.

HOPE (*off*). So I couldn't get through to my sister but I'm sure it's – (*Enters.*)

Beat.

Um –

OFFICER (*struggling*). *FUCK.*

ALI (*to* ISLA). Uh, what do you wanna do now?

ISLA. Hope, take the baby outside, will you? I'm gonna kill the cunt.

HOPE. But –

ISLA. Here, take him.

HOPE. No.

ISLA. What?

HOPE. No don't do it.

ISLA. Take the fucking baby, Hope.

HOPE. *No.*

ISLA. Are you joking? If it wasn't for him Becca would be alive.

HOPE. It won't help.

ISLA. But it will – it *will* help cos otherwise he'll be chasing us our whole lives.

OFFICER. I won't, I promise – I'll –

ISLA. Shut up.

Beat.

HOPE. Fine. (*Takes baby.*) You'll regret it though. (*Leaves.*)

ISLA *straightens arm, gun pointed at* POLICE OFFICER*'s head.*

OFFICER (*wriggling, struggling*). *Wait* –

ISLA *closes her eyes.*

Pause.

She opens her eyes and lowers the gun.

ISLA. Shit.

OFFICER (*sighs in relief*).

   Beat.

ALI. There's – um, quite a lot of rope in my bag.

   Beat.

   If that's helpful.

   Blackout.

*

Darkness.

Sound of a river.

*

Darkness.

Sound of mountain breeze.

*

Darkness.

Sound of rainy night.

*

Darkness.

Sound of dawn.

*

A field.

WAYNE *is blindfolded and restrained by ropes.*

HOPE. Um –

ISLA. Are we lost, Hope?

HOPE. No.

ISLA. No?

HOPE. No, no –

ISLA. Because we seem lost.

HOPE. No it's somewhere near here, I'm sure of it.

WAYNE. I do think I need to go to a hospital.

ISLA. Shut up.

HOPE. Wait, it's over this fence.

ISLA. Are you sure?

HOPE. Yeah, definitely. It's over this fence and then it's –

LOR appears behind them with a shotgun.

LOR. STOP.

Beat.

Move a fucking muscle and you'll get a shotgun shell to the face.

They go to turn around.

No *don't* turn around, that's moving.

ALI. Sorry.

LOR. What are you here for? You're trespassing.

HOPE. We're um – looking for the Strawberry Fields Commune?

LOR. It's gone.

HOPE. What?

LOR. It's *gone*. It doesn't exist any more. Now fuck off back the way you came please and –

HOPE. Wait. (*Turns.*) Lor? (*Approaches.*) Lor, it's – it's – it's me.

The others turn and watch.

Hope.

LOR *keeps shotgun on* HOPE.

Pause.

She lowers it, sighs, then turns and exits.

Blackout.

4.

Morning.

A worn-down farmhouse kitchen.

HOPE, ISLA (*with baby*), ALI, *and* WAYNE (*blindfolded and restrained*) *are sat around dining table finishing soup.* ISLA *occasionally feeds baby some soup.*

'We'll Meet Again' by Vera Lynn is playing on a small CD player.

LOR *enters smoking a cigarette and using a mug as ashtray. She sits at the table.*

ALI. Um, it's a lovely soup.

LOR. Thanks.

ALI. Is it home-made?

LOR. What?

ALI. You know, made using veg from the vegetable garden?

LOR. Oh no it's Tescos.

ALI. Oh.

LOR. The veg garden's still fucked.

WAYNE. Um, can I have another mouthful, please?

ALI *feeds* WAYNE *soup.*

HOPE. So, what actually happened?

LOR. To the commune?

HOPE. Yeah.

LOR (*shrugs*). What always happens. You know – burnout, betrayal, dwindling resources, an incident involving BP's private army… the usual.

HOPE. Oh.

LOR. It's alright though.

HOPE. Is it?

LOR. Yeah. I mean everything dies eventually, doesn't it?

Pause.

I might have a glass of wine. Anyone want one?

ALI. Now?

LOR. Yeah.

ALI. It's quarter-past *ten*.

LOR. So?

ALI. Oh, I uh – was just saying in case anyone wanted to know the time.

Beat.

It's quarter-past ten.

LOR *gets up and pours herself a large glass of wine.*

HOPE. Actually, um – do you mind if I chat to Lor alone?

ALI. Oh, uh –

ISLA (*getting up*). No, course.

ALI (*getting up*). Could probably do with some sleep anyway.

LOR. You can take any of the bedrooms upstairs.

ISLA. Cool.

LOR. And there's a basement downstairs.

Beat.

For the pig.

ISLA. Ah.

LOR. And speaking of pigs, I'm not gonna have his friends turning up at my door, am I?

ALI. No –

ISLA *and* ALI *start to leave with* WAYNE.

WAYNE (*being dragged off*). Wait, don't take me to the basement – I'm not gonna try anything. Wait, stop… *stop…*

They leave.

LOR *turns the CD player off and necks her glass of wine.*

LOR. Quite the circus you've brought to my house, so – thank you.

Pours another glass.

HOPE *(stands)*. Lor, what the fuck are you doing?

LOR. What the fuck am *I* doing? What the fuck are *you* doing? I've not seen you in twenty-odd years and you've just turned up at my house with no notice and a fucking ticking time-bomb of fucking very chaotic shit!

HOPE. Yeah but I did *try* and give you notice – I've been trying to call you.

LOR. Since when?

HOPE. Since arriving two days ago.

LOR. Oh. Well, I don't use my phone any more, so –

HOPE. What about *this* then?

LOR. About what?

HOPE. Um, the fucking morning wine? How long's *that* been a thing?

LOR. Oh you're one to judge.

HOPE. Come on –

LOR. I never judged *you*.

HOPE. Yeah fine but that's different.

LOR. Why?

HOPE. Because *we're* different. I'm the flighty fuck-up and you're the one who gets things done – you know, who *does* shit – makes things better.

LOR *(smirks)*.

HOPE. What? Am I not allowed to worry about you?

LOR. *Worry* about me? Hope, I was eighteen when you left me with your baby to raise and then fucked off and disappeared. And you didn't even ask me either! You let me find out from the store manager of a fucking McDonald's and a note on a fucking napkin! 'Worried' about me – go fuck yourself. You know, you and your new friends and prisoner can stay here, that's fine. But don't you dare pretend to care about me or anything other than your-fucking-self, alright? (*Picks up bottle*.) Now *I'm* gonna go and spend the rest of the day in my room. For dinner there should be a bunch of ready meals in the freezer. Help yourselves. (*Starts to leave*.)

HOPE. Wait, Lor.

LOR (*doesn't stop*).

HOPE. Lor, what happened to him – to Mitch?

LOR (*doesn't stop*).

HOPE. Where is he?

LOR (*doesn't stop*).

HOPE. Lor.

LOR (*about to leave*).

HOPE. *Lor.*

LOR (*leaves*).

    Pause.

    HOPE *sits down*.

*

ISLA (*with baby*) *and* ALI *enter*.

ISLA. Morning –

ALI. Morning –

HOPE. Morning.

ISLA. You sleep alright?

HOPE. Yeah. Yeah, I mean a bit.

    Beat.

    You?

ISLA. Like a log. This place is fucking lush.

HOPE. Yeah.

ISLA. Falling apart obviously but still.

ALI. We just went on a morning stroll around the land.

HOPE. Did you?

ISLA. Yeah. Forest nerd over here's getting all hard about starting a new veg garden.

ALI. Well, it sort of depends on how long we're staying here.

HOPE. I think you can stay here as long as you like.

ISLA. Really?

HOPE. Yeah I mean you can ask Lor yourself but it's what she said, basically. She doesn't seem bothered.

ALI. Cool.

ISLA. How long are *you* staying?

HOPE. I don't know yet.

ISLA. But at least a week though, right?

HOPE. Probably.

ISLA. Cos we were thinking about doing a shop.

ALI. Lor said I could borrow her car, so.

HOPE. Did she?

ALI. Yeah, just now. We bumped into her on the walk.

HOPE. Oh.

ALI. Also gonna try get some seeds.

ISLA. See, I told you! He can't fucking help himself.

WAYNE (*off, from basement*). OI!

    Beat.

    ANYONE? I NEED A FUCKING *SHIT*!

ALI. I'll go.

ISLA. You sure?

ALI. Yeah.

ISLA. How you gonna do it?

ALI. I dunno. Bucket? Keep the gun on him?

ISLA. Yeah don't untie him though.

ALI. No.

WAYNE (*off, from basement*). *OI!*

ISLA. SOMEONE'S COMING!

ALI (*takes gun from table drawer*). See you in a bit.

ISLA. Good luck.

> ALI *leaves*.
>
> ISLA *waits for* ALI *to be clearly out of earshot*.
>
> *Beat*.
>
> Fuck, Hope, this is the best adventure *ever*. I've met an actual nice guy who loves wholesome stuff like trees, I've temporarily sorted the Wayne problem... it's the best.

HOPE. I'm glad.

ISLA. What's wrong?

HOPE. Nothing.

ISLA. Fuck off, Hope, what *is* it?

HOPE. Nothing, it's just – well, you know before when I told you Lor was expecting me and then also when I told you I rang her and that she was expecting you *too*?

ISLA. Yeah?

HOPE. Those were lies.

ISLA. I know.

HOPE. Oh.

ISLA. I realised.

HOPE. Right. Well, the thing is our relationship is a bit broken and one of the main reasons I came here – came to the Republic was to try and mend it, you know?

ISLA. Sure.

HOPE. But she's not letting me even *try*.

ISLA. Okay, but it's only been a night, Hope. These things take time.

HOPE. You think?

ISLA. Yes. Just keep just being here and let her come to *you*.

HOPE. Alright. Um, thank you.

ISLA (*nods*).

*

Sound of front door opening.

ISLA. Oh that'll be Ali with the shopping.

Sound of front door closing.

ALI *enters with several shopping bags.*

Alright?

ALI. Alright?

ISLA. You manage to get everything?

ALI. Pretty much.

ISLA. And no sign of a search party or anything?

ALI. No.

ISLA. Okay, good.

ALI *puts bags down and returns the gun to the kitchen drawer.*

Who's cooking tonight then?

ALI. *I* can.

ISLA. Nah. You went to the shop and helped Wayne shit.

ALI. But I don't mind, really.

ISLA. You sure?

ALI. Yeah. It's just nice like *wanting* to do stuff again, you know?

Beat.

I'll do the sweet potato curry.

Starts unpacking bags.

ISLA. Okay. I'll do tomorrow then –

HOPE. And I can do the day after.

ISLA. What was yours again?

HOPE. A Bolognese?

ISLA. Oh yeah. Hang on, I'll make a rota.

ALI. There's paper and pens in this drawer here, I think. (*Looks*.) Yeah.

Takes out paper and a pen. Passes to ISLA.

Here you go.

ISLA. Ta. Right – Tuesday's Ali, Wednesday's me, Thursday's Hope –

HOPE. Yep.

ISLA. Who wants to do Friday?

LOR (*appears at doorway, holding two empty bottles of wine*). I can do it.

ISLA. Oh, uh – no. No, *you* shouldn't have to cook.

ALI. Yeah it's your house.

LOR. No, I *want* to.

ISLA. Um, okay.

LOR (*crossing kitchen*). Put me down to cook whatever.

ISLA. Let me check what's left. Uh, goulash?

LOR (*puts bottles in recycling bin*). Goulash is fine.

ISLA. Right you're Friday then, Lor.

LOR (*nods. Crossing back*). You can do a cleaning rota too, if you want.

ISLA. Oh, sure.

LOR. But keep me off that one, yeah? With the house privileges. Also next time you're doing a shop use the debit card in the drawer there.

ISLA. What? No, we're not gonna use *your* money.

LOR. No it's alright. There's like twenty grand on it from the BP settlement. I was saving it in case I ever wanted to set up another so – just use it, okay?

ISLA. I –

LOR. *Okay?*

ISLA. Okay, okay.

> LOR *nods and leaves*.

*

Afternoon.

Baby is crying.

ISLA. It's okay, Isaac. Um, I'm gonna go try and calm him down.

> LOR *enters*.

(*Leaving*.) Oh hey, Lor. You still okay doing the goulash tonight?

LOR. Course, yeah.

ISLA. Can't wait.

> *Beat*.

LOR. Hi.

HOPE. Hi.

> *Beat*.

ALI. Um, I'm gonna go and plant some more seeds.

LOR. Okay.

ALI. See youse in a bit.

HOPE. See you.

LOR. Bye.

> ALI *leaves*.
>
> *Pause*.

Wine?

HOPE. Oh, um –

LOR. Don't check your watch, it's gone three o'clock!

HOPE (*smiles*). Okay then.

> LOR *nods. Crosses kitchen and starts pouring two glasses of wine.*

LOR. So uh what's it like being back here? At Strawberry's.

HOPE. Oh, um –

LOR. Different?

HOPE. Well, yeah.

LOR. Cos the last time you were here would've been – well, Strawberry's at its peak, right?

HOPE. I still think it's great though.

LOR (*smirks*). Do you?

> *Brings glasses over and sits.*

HOPE. Yeah but – it's just nice seeing you.

> *Beat.*

> Hey, uh – do you remember that joke Mum used to tell about the clown and the angel?

LOR. Obviously. She'd tell it all the fucking time.

HOPE. Well, I told it to a guy on the plane over here and not only did he already know it but he said I told it wrong.

LOR. Really? Why?

HOPE. Cos I changed Maurice's name to Hope.

LOR. Of course you did.

> *Beat.*

> Well, he's right, it's not as good.

HOPE. I knew you'd say that.

LOR. Cig?

HOPE. Go on then.

LOR *takes out two cigarettes, passes one to* HOPE.

Ta.

They light them and smoke.

Pause.

HOPE. Is Mum – um –

LOR. Dead?

HOPE. Yeah.

LOR. Yeah.

Beat.

Nine years now.

HOPE. What was the funeral like?

LOR. Shit. No one fucking *came*. It was just me and a few
nurses from the hospice.

HOPE. What about her friends?

LOR. What friends?

HOPE. Our dads then?

LOR. No. I mean *my* dad was long dead by then.

HOPE. Sorry –

LOR. And your dad *wasn't* but didn't come.

HOPE. Oh.

LOR. But is now.

Beat.

Dead.

HOPE. Right.

LOR. I'd say sorry for being the bearer of all this death news
but it's your fault you didn't know, so…

Beat.

HOPE. And Mitch?

LOR. Fuck off, Hope.

HOPE. What?

LOR. No I'm not ready to talk to you about him – not yet.

HOPE. But –

LOR. Look, if I ever tell you about Mitch it's not gonna be in the first fucking week I've *seen* you in twenty years, alright? It's gonna be when I trust you – when I know you're not gonna just fuck back off again. So if all you want from me is Mitch's phone number, then you might as well as just leave. But if you actually want to be here – actually want to start making up for all your fucking shit then take it as a win that I want to get drunk with you.

Beat.

HOPE. Fine. (*Necks her glass.*) Let's get drunk.

                              *

Evening.

LOR *pours* HOPE *another glass.*

Both cackling drunkenly.

HOPE. And then he said –

HOPE *and* LOR. '*Sorry*, Mrs Seagrave, but I think you've shat on my geraniums!'

Cackling.

HOPE. Her face –

LOR. It was priceless. (*Finishes pouring.*)

HOPE. And then after, when she – when she, um –

   ISLA (*without baby*) *and* ALI *enter.*

ISLA *and* ALI. Hey!

HOPE *and* LOR. *Hey!*

ISLA. Another one of *these* nights, is it?

LOR (*drunken shrug*).

ISLA. Is there food?

HOPE. Yeah.

LOR. It's Hope's night but we knew we were gonna get pissed and there was still my frozen goulash from weeks ago so I defrosted it. Just need to heat it up when you're hungry.

ISLA. Great –

ALI. Thanks.

HOPE. Where've you been today?

ISLA. Just out and about. Look what we got though. (*Shows baby monitor.*)

LOR. Nice.

ISLA. I had one before but left it when we went on the run, so.

HOPE. Means you don't have to worry at night – you know, like if you two want to spend time together at night *without* the baby and –

LOR (*giggles*).

ISLA. Shut up.

ALI (*blushes*).

Pause.

HOPE. Um –

LOR. Shit, I forgot to show you something.

HOPE. Really?

LOR. In the lounge, yeah.

HOPE. Right.

Both get up and leave.

ISLA and ALI smile awkwardly.

ISLA puts the baby monitor on the table.

ISLA. Sorry.

ALI. Why are you saying sorry?

ISLA. I dunno. I guess I didn't want you to think that –

ALI *kisses* ISLA.

ISLA *is taken by surprise but then kisses him back.*

*

Night.

ISLA *and* ALI *are sat, intertwined.*

Sound of HOPE *and* LOR *stumbling downstairs and giggling.*

LOR (*off, from corridor*). Right, we're ready!

ISLA. Okay.

HOPE (*off, from corridor*). Cue the music –

ALI. The music's cued.

LOR (*off, from corridor*). Then let me present, to perform your 'Strawberry Fields Three Months' *Anniversary* Dance', it's Hope and Lor!

ALI *presses play on CD player.*

A big-band or jazz-orchestra song plays.

HOPE *and* LOR *dance drunkenly into the room wearing child-sized pink tutus. They perform a routine they've clearly just been practising. They giggle throughout.*

ISLA. Oh my god. Where did you get all that?

LOR. From the loft!

HOPE. They're the ones we had as kids!

ISLA. So stupid.

LOR. Right, remember the thing – remember the *thing…*

They continue performing as ALI *and* ISLA *watch on smiling, clearly moved and finding it ridiculous. When* HOPE *and* LOR *run out of routine they start to dance arm-in-arm.* ALI *and* ISLA *do the same and all four dance. By the end they're no longer giggling, clearly all finding it emotional for different reasons. Perhaps this sequence takes place over two different pieces of music.*

After a couple of minutes or so faint banging can be heard from basement.

ALI. Wait, *stop* – stop. Can you hear that?

ISLA. Hear what?

ALI *turns music off.*

Loud banging and grunts from basement.

Beat.

ALI. He's out the ropes.

HOPE. What?

ALI. He's got loose – he's trying to barge through the door.

A particularly loud bang and grunt from basement.

ISLA. Fuck, um – what do we do?

ALI. I guess go down with the gun and try and tie him up again?

ISLA. Should I come too?

ALI *(takes gun from the drawer).* Probably, yeah.

HOPE. Do you want us to come, or –

ALI. No, no we should be okay. Just listen out in case.

LOR. Course.

ALI *and* ISLA *leave.*

HOPE *and* LOR *stay standing.*

Banging continues then sound of a ruckus downstairs.

WAYNE *(off, from basement).* Fuck – *fuck.*

Goes quiet.

Simultaneously, sensing the situation is being handled, they both go and sit down.

Pause.

LOR. More wine?

HOPE. Yeah.

*

LOR. More wine?

*

HOPE. More wine?

*

LOR. More wine?

*

Early hours of morning.

LOR *flops down towards the table.*

Pause.

HOPE. More wine?

LOR. No.

HOPE. One more.

LOR (*flopping back up*). Nope. I need to go to bed.

HOPE. Alright.

LOR. Had a great night though.

HOPE. Yeah?

LOR. Yeah. Just wish we'd had more of them, you know?

HOPE. What do you mean?

LOR. You know, when we were young.

HOPE. Yeah but there's plenty of time, isn't there? Or *some* time, anyway.

LOR. True. Yeah better late than never, I guess.

HOPE. Exactly.

    Beat.

LOR. Anyway. (*Stands.*) Goodnight, Hope.

HOPE. Night.

LOR. I'll see you in the morning.

    LOR *goes to leave.*

HOPE. Uh – *wait*, um… Lor?

Stands.

LOR (*stopping*). Yeah?

HOPE. Before you go, can you tell me something about Mitch?

LOR (*sighs*).

HOPE. Just one thing – just *any*thing, just – please?

LOR. No.

HOPE. Why? Cos I get why you didn't at first – you know, like when I'd just arrived but it's been three months now. Haven't I proven that I *do* care? About you? About Mitch?

LOR. Why, because you've stayed with me for three whole months?

HOPE. Well –

LOR. Because we've got pissed together a few times? Because we did a stupid dance in our childhood fucking tutus then that just makes up for it all, does it? I'm just supposed to forgive you now?

HOPE. No you don't have to forgive me, just tell me where he *is*.

LOR. I don't *know* where he is.

HOPE. Really?

LOR. No. And you know why? Why he ran away and stopped speaking to me?

HOPE. I –

LOR. Because of *you*. Because he found out about you.

HOPE. What do you *mean* 'found out about me'?

LOR. I mean at fifteen he found out through a kid at school that his mum abandoned him in a McDonald's.

HOPE. But what did he think before?

LOR. That you were dead.

HOPE. I'm *sorry*?

LOR. I panicked! What was I supposed to say? I mean when he was really little it didn't matter but eventually he started asking questions. And at first I just said you were gone but he pushed and pushed and so, when he asked if you were dead –

HOPE. You said *yes*?

LOR. You might as well have been! And it felt much nicer than telling him you just fucking left him. But when he found out he was so angry – so heartbroken. So then he left.

Beat.

HOPE. And you haven't seen him since?

LOR. No.

HOPE. What, you didn't even *try* looking for him or –

LOR *throws glass at* HOPE *– misses, smashes behind her.*

LOR. Yes I fucking looked for him and I didn't wait twenty-four fucking years to *do* it, you fucking selfish fucking *deluded* fucking cu–

Baby starts crying on monitor.

Long pause.

ISLA (*voice, on monitor*). *Hey.* Hey it's okay. Mummy's got you. Mummy's got you. Shall I sing? Do you want me to sing, Isaac?

Clears throat. Sings first verse of 'We'll Meet Again'. Starts singing second verse.

LOR (*turns baby monitor off*). When I wake up tomorrow I want you gone. (*Leaves.*)

Beat.

HOPE *sits down, dejected. She finishes half-drunk glasses of wine on table.*

Sound of giant's footsteps.

Beat.

HOPE. Hello?

Game-show theme tune plays through baby monitor.

CLOWN (*voice-over, from baby monitor*). Gooooood evening. Are you ready for Round Two, Hope?

HOPE *cowers down on table, hands on head.*

(*Whispering.*) Hope. Hope.

*

Morning.

HOPE *is asleep, head on table.*

ISLA (*with baby*) and ALI *stand near.*

ISLA. *Hope.*

HOPE (*gasps*).

ISLA. Good morning.

ALI. Morning.

HOPE. Did I sleep down here?

ISLA. Looks like it.

HOPE. Oh.

ISLA. Uh – listen, sorry to wake you but we're heading off now so just checking you're still okay to drive and pick up the door locks and camera and bike chains and stuff?

Beat.

HOPE. What?

ISLA. Um – don't you remember?

HOPE. No?

ISLA. It's just last night you offered to go out and get the stuff to make the whole basement situation more secure cos me and Ali had a sort of day trip planned for today. A hike-and-picnic type thing?

HOPE. Oh. Yeah I don't remember that at all.

ISLA. Well, is it still fine?

HOPE. Um… maybe you should ask Lor instead.

ISLA. We were *gonna*, when we saw you were asleep, but she's
gone – she's not in the house and the thing is we sort of need
to leave now if we want to get to the top of the BP Peak and
back before night.

HOPE. Right.

ALI. But I mean, if it's *not* fine I can always go and we can do
the hike another day, or –

ISLA *shoots* ALI *a look*.

HOPE. No, no, I can do it.

ISLA. Are you sure?

HOPE. Yeah.

ALI. You don't have to set any of it up but –

HOPE. No I can do that too.

ALI. Really?

ISLA. Thanks.

ALI. Thank you. I'll um – put the car keys here on the table.

HOPE. Cheers.

ALI. And the gun's in the drawer.

HOPE (*nods*).

ISLA. See you tonight then!

HOPE. Bye.

ALI. Bye.

ISLA *and* ALI *leave*.

Sound of them leaving through front door.

Pause.

HOPE *takes cigarette from packet on the table.*

She's about to light it.

WAYNE (*off, from basement*). HELLO?

HOPE *stops*.

IS ANYONE THERE? I NEED A *PISS*.

Beat.

HELLO?

Beat.

HEL-*LO*-O.

HOPE *sighs and puts the cigarette behind ear.*

HEL–

HOPE. YEAH, ONE *SECOND*.

Blackout.

*

A basement.

WAYNE *is tied to a chair by his hands, legs and waist. His pants and trousers are at his ankles and his blindfold is on his forehead.* HOPE *holds the gun in one hand. With the other hand she holds a metal bucket under* WAYNE*'s crotch. She takes the bucket and places it near the door. She returns to him and pulls up his pants and trousers. She reaches for his blindfold to pull it down.*

WAYNE. Wait, I uh – I don't suppose I can have some of that fag, can I?

Beat.

Please? I'm not saying unfasten me or anything, just light it and hold it to my mouth. I just haven't had one since I got here and I'm fucking gasping.

HOPE. Um –

WAYNE. Fucking *please*, Hope, I –

HOPE. Fine, hold on.

WAYNE. Thanks.

HOPE *takes a chair from the side of the room and brings it opposite* WAYNE. *She sits, lights it, has a few drags, then holds it to* WAYNE*'s mouth so he can smoke. After two* *drags, she leans back into her chair, puts the lighter on the floor, and smokes.*

I appreciate that.

HOPE (*nods*).

WAYNE. And you sitting with me. I've just spent so long in my own head, you know? And I'm not saying I don't deserve it, I'm just… lonely.

Pause.

So, uh – what was all that noise last night?

HOPE. What noise?

WAYNE. I dunno. I heard banging and shouting and glass breaking.

HOPE. Oh. (*Leans in to give* WAYNE *a drag.*) It was nothing.

WAYNE. Was it? (*Takes drag.*) Didn't sound like it. (*Takes another drag.*) Sounded like you and Lor were fighting about something.

HOPE (*leans back*). Why do *you* care? (*Takes drag.*)

WAYNE. I *don't*. But I've got nothing fucking else to think about down here, do I?

HOPE. True. (*Takes drag.*) We were fighting about my son.

WAYNE. Your son?

HOPE (*nods. Leans forward*). Mitch.

WAYNE. Oh. (*Takes drag.*) I didn't know you had a son. (*Takes drag.*)

HOPE. I sort of abandoned him. Left him for Lor to raise.

WAYNE. I'm sure you had your reasons.

HOPE. I did. I *did* have my reasons. But we were fighting cos, when I asked where he was, she wouldn't tell me. Said she didn't know. (*Takes drag.*)

WAYNE. Didn't know?

HOPE. No.

WAYNE. That sounds like bullshit.

HOPE. Maybe. (*Leans in*.) I think I believe her though. She says when he found out that I wasn't dead – that I was alive but had just *left* him, he ran away. And she did say she looked for him but never found him.

WAYNE. Mm. (*Takes drag*.) And who's his dad?

HOPE. What?

WAYNE. Who's his *dad*?

HOPE. Um, Roy. My ex-husband.

Beat.

Why?

WAYNE. Just saying cos, if it was *me* in that situation, first thing I'd do is look for my dad. You know, a boy fucking needs his dad. And if I found out that the person I always thought was my mum had lied, that my real mum had *left* me, I'd immediately go looking for –

HOPE *puts out cigarette and stands up*.

Hope?

HOPE *goes to leave*.

Wait, Hope.

HOPE *leaves, closing and locking door behind her.*

Pause.

WAYNE *notices the lighter on floor.*

He shimmies his chair so he's right above it.

Blackout.

*

Darkness.

A lighter flicks into life.

5.

A middle-class, suburban living room.

HOPE *and* NEW WIFE *are sat on sofa as far apart as possible.*

On the coffee table there are two cups of tea.

'Concerto No. 1, "Spring": Allegro' by Antonio Vivaldi is playing on the radio.

Pause.

NEW WIFE. He shouldn't be long now.

HOPE. Cool.

    Beat.

NEW WIFE. It's funny, you don't look at all like how I'd imagined.

HOPE. Really?

NEW WIFE. No.

HOPE. What did you imagine?

NEW WIFE. I don't know. I guess I forgot you were so much older than me.

HOPE. Mm.

    Beat.

    And – sorry, what was your name again?

NEW WIFE. Pandora.

HOPE. Right.

NEW WIFE. Oh because I suppose you didn't *know* Roy had remarried?

HOPE. No I didn't give a fuck.

    Pause.

    NEW WIFE *checks watch.*

    Beat.

NEW WIFE. You know, I think I might just try calling him again.

HOPE. Alright.

NEW WIFE. I'll get some biscuits as well.

HOPE. Thanks.

NEW WIFE *leaves*.

*

A hallway, just outside the living room.

PANDORA *enters on the phone. A beep of an answerphone.*

PANDORA. Hi, it's me again. Please call me back as soon as possible, please. It's urgent. And if it turns out you're in the *pub* again, I'll –

ROY (EX-HUSBAND) *enters*.

Oh.

ROY. Hello.

PANDORA. Hello.

Beat.

You haven't checked your phone, have you?

ROY. No?

PANDORA. Guess who's in the living room?

ROY. Who?

PANDORA. *Guess.*

Beat.

Your ex-wife.

ROY. What the fuck?

PANDORA. *Language*, Roy.

ROY. Sorry.

ROY *leaves*.

*

The living room.

ROY *enters followed by* PANDORA.

Beat.

ROY. Hello.

HOPE. Hi.

Beat.

ROY. Um –

PANDORA. Tea?

ROY. Please.

PANDORA. Hope? Another tea?

HOPE. No thank you.

PANDORA (*smiles. Leaves*).

Beat.

ROY (*whispering*). What the fuck are you doing?

HOPE. Sit down.

ROY. Um… okay.

Approaches and sits.

Beat.

What do you want?

HOPE. I'm looking for Mitch and I know you know where he is.

ROY. What? I *don't* know where he is.

HOPE. You do.

ROY. I don't.

HOPE. You *do*.

ROY. Hope, I really don't, I –

HOPE (*pulling out gun and pointing it at* ROY). Where the fuck is he, Roy?

ROY. Whoa. (*Puts hands up.*) Look – easy, Hope – *easy…*

PANDORA (*voice, from hall*). Right. Roy, your tea will be a few minutes but here's a gourmet collection of biscuits I bought from –

Enters with tray of biscuits. Sees HOPE *pointing gun at* ROY.

Beat.

PANDORA *screams and drops the biscuits.*

She runs back out the room.

HOPE (*standing*). Oi! Get the fuck back in here or Roy gets it in the face. I'll count from three. Three, two, *one* –

PANDORA *enters.*

Now shut the door, turn that radio off and come and sit down.

PANDORA *shuts the door and turns radio off.*

Quickly.

PANDORA *rushes over and sits next to* ROY *on sofa.*

Thank you.

PANDORA. You can't take Roy back at gunpoint!

HOPE. Yeah that's not what I'm doing. So look, basically, I'm trying to find my son and it's recently come to my attention that when he was fifteen Mitch ran away from Lor and that she hasn't seen him since. And, thinking about it, the obvious place he'd run away *to* is here. So, I'm gonna ask you again Roy. Where the fuck is he?

ROY. I – I – I mean it's true, he *did* come here.

HOPE. Did he?

ROY. Yes –

PANDORA. Yes –

ROY. *Yes*, he came here asking to stay –

PANDORA. And he *did* stay –

ROY. He did stay yes, for – what, like six months?

PANDORA. Five-and-a-half months, yes –

ROY. Five-and-a-half months.

HOPE. And *then*?

ROY. Well, when he arrived asking to stay I obviously said yes –
I was happy for him to because I knew you were away and that
he had no one *else*. But the thing is – well, Pandora here was
less, um –

PANDORA. No *I* was happy to –

ROY. Well –

PANDORA. I fucking *was*, Roy, but the thing is we had our
own boys –

ROY. That's true –

PANDORA. Hugo and Bruno, and it was all a bit of a handful –

ROY. It *was* a handful, actually –

PANDORA. Especially as Mitch and our boys didn't really get
on that well.

ROY. No, and Mitch was very *angry* – very upset.

PANDORA. With you, Hope –

ROY. Not just you –

PANDORA. There were a few incidents, a few uh –

ROY. Behavioural incidents –

PANDORA. Involving drugs –

ROY. Not drugs –

PANDORA. Well, involving *achohol* then.

ROY. Yes –

PANDORA. So eventually, I did say to Roy that maybe he
should find somewhere else to live –

ROY. And then I spoke to *Mitch* and then he left.

    Beat.

HOPE. That's *it*?

ROY. Yes –

PANDORA. Yes.

HOPE. You never spoke to him again?

ROY. Well, we tried –

PANDORA. You tried to reach out, didn't you?

ROY. I did – I called him a few times but he never answered.
    And then the third or fourth time I tried it said the number
    didn't exist… so I stopped.

   Beat.

HOPE. Oh.

   Beat.

   HOPE *lowers gun.*

   Pause.

ROY. So, um – is that, um – *everything* then, or –

HOPE. What? Oh, yeah – yeah, I'll get going.

ROY. *Great.*

HOPE. But uh – thanks for the tea and biscuits.

PANDORA. You're welcome.

HOPE. Yeah, uh – bye, then. (*Goes to leave.*)

PANDORA. Bye –

ROY. Bye –

PANDORA. *Bye –*

   HOPE *leaves.*

   PANDORA *and* ROY *remain seated, still and shell-shocked.*

   Sound of HOPE *leaving through front door.*

   Sound of door closing.

   Blackout.

                            *

A park in the rain.

HOPE *is sat on a bench.*

HOPE. Mum?

   Beat.

I uh – know I'm just in a park and not at your grave, cos
I don't actually know where your grave is, but I'm thinking
that if I'm wrong and some sort of afterlife *does* exist,
presumably you're not bound to the location you're buried
in, right? Like, if you were able to hear me there, you can
hear me *here*, is what I'm thinking. So, um – I'm just gonna
say it and hope for the best, alright?

Beat.

I'm sorry. For leaving you – for leaving you and Lor and
Mitch. It just felt too hard, you know? And maybe it's meant
to – maybe you're *meant* to find it hard and you just have to
deal with it but *I* couldn't.

Beat.

So I'm sorry and I love you…

Beat.

Bye.

Pause.

ANGEL *enters, pulls their angel onesie down to his ankles
and starts pissing into a hedge. He finishes, approaches and
sits next to* HOPE *on the bench.*

Beat.

ANGEL. Alright?

HOPE. Alright?

Beat.

Do you always dress like that, or –

ANGEL. Oh, no I'm on a stag do.

HOPE. Oh.

ANGEL. Or I *was* but then I went out for a phone call and then
my phone died and then, when I went back into the pub,
everyone was gone, so –

HOPE. Sorry.

ANGEL. S'okay.

Pause.

I heard you talking to your dead mum.

Beat.

I have a dead mum.

HOPE. Do you?

ANGEL. Yeah. And the stuff you were saying – the stuff about whether it's supposed to feel this hard, *I* think that. I think that every day. Especially at the moment cos I've got a two-year-old and a four-year-old, and my mum died last year, and I was recently made redundant from Koka Kola Railways so I'm looking for a new job whilst being proper worried about affording food and bills and rent. And then I worry about climate change, and I worry about fascists, and I worry about how fucking cruel this world is and also I think I'm a piece of shit.

Beat.

So, what I was thinking when I was listening to you and pissing in that hedge over there, is that I don't know if it's *meant* to be too hard but what I do know is that I'm finding it too hard too. And if I'm finding it too hard, and you're finding it too hard, we can't be the only ones, can we?

HOPE. No.

ANGEL. No.

Beat.

And also – oh shit, that's my groom.

GROOM (*voice-over*). Barry!

ANGEL. I'm coming.

GROOM (*voice-over*). BARRY!

ANGEL. I'M *COMING*! (*Stands.*) Well, uh – hang on in there.

HOPE. You too.

ANGEL *leaves.*

Sound of giant's footsteps.

*

The kitchen.

ISLA *is standing.*

ALI *enters.*

ALI. Any sign of her?

ISLA. No.

ALI. Couldn't see Lor anywhere outside either. It's a bit weird.

ISLA. Is it?

ALI. Maybe not.

ISLA. Maybe they're together?

ALI. Maybe but then where's the car?

ISLA. True. Well, maybe Hope came back, sorted the basement and then together they went off to –

WAYNE (*off, from basement*). HELLO?

   Beat.

   OI! I KNOW SOMEONE'S THERE.

ISLA. Fucksake.

WAYNE (*off, from basement*). HELLO-O? NO ONE'S BROUGHT ME ANY FOOD ALL DAY!

ISLA. Alright.

WAYNE (*off, from basement*). I'M FUCKING STARVING.

ISLA. *ALRIGHT*. WE'LL BRING SOMETHING DOWN NOW.

ALI. I'll go.

ISLA. You sure?

ALI. Yeah it's all good. I'm just gonna take him the leftover picnic crisps.

ISLA. Okay.

ALI (*goes to drawer*). The gun's not here.

ISLA. Really?

ALI. No.

ISLA. Oh, uh –

ALI. Hope's probably still got it.

ISLA. Probably. What you gonna do?

ALI. I've got the knife.

ISLA. Really? You sure you don't want to wait until –

ALI. Nah it'll be okay.

ISLA. Okay.

Beat.

Well, I uh – had a lovely time today.

ALI. Me too.

ISLA. Like, really lovely.

ALI. Me *too*.

Both grin.

WAYNE (*off, from basement*). OI!

ALI. Anyway, uh – won't be long.

ALI leaves.

ISLA sits down. She picks up the baby monitor from the table and turns it on. The baby can be heard making little noises. ISLA smiles.

*

Later.

Footsteps approaching.

ISLA (*she starts to turn towards door*). All good or –

WAYNE is standing at the doorway holding a bloodied knife.

WAYNE. Where's my boy?

Baby starts crying on the monitor.

Beat.

WAYNE moves as if going to go and get the baby but ISLA runs at him, trying to pry the knife from his hand.

WAYNE *overpowers her and pushes her towards the table.*

With one hand he pins ISLA *down on the table. He raises the knife above his head.*

This is your fault!

ISLA *is trying but struggling to break free.*

Do you hear me? This is *your* fucking fault!

HOPE *enters holding the gun.*

She has it pointed at WAYNE *but doesn't fire.*

ISLA *sees her.*

ISLA. Hope?

WAYNE. I'm sorry.

He's about to bring the knife down and kill her.

ISLA (*closing her eyes*). Hope –

WAYNE. I'm *sorry*, I just –

Gunshot.

WAYNE *dies.*

Silence.

HOPE *stays still apart from her hand which is shaking.*

Sound of waves gently hitting the shore.

HOPE *lowers the gun.*

Blackout.

6.

Darkness.

Sound of waves continues.

REPORTER (*voice-over*). And tonight's main story is the false
    imprisonment and brutal murder of police officer Wayne
    Cartwright. Prime suspects include a transgender waitress,
    a communist and former commune leader, a forest ranger
    who is believed to be deceased, and a woman called Hope.
    Earlier we spoke to the nation's CEO Brendan Martin about
    how he intends to address the matter.

CEO (*voice-over*). Well, I can assure you that everything is
    being done to find and apprehend the culprits of this horrific,
    violent crime. However, what I'd like to do *now*, is pay
    tribute to the brave and honourable police officer whose life
    was cut short. It is my belief that *without* people like Wayne
    Cartwright, the People's Republic of Koka Kola would be
    less than half the brilliant and successful country it is today.
    And it is for this reason that I intend to introduce a new
    public holiday in his honour. From now on every year on the
    fourteenth of October we will celebrate Wayne Cartwright
    and grieve a man who stood for duty, integrity and –

*   *

A pebbled beach.

HOPE, LOR *and* ISLA (*holding baby*) *are sat on the stones.*

All three wear lifejackets.

Pause.

ISLA. So um – do we have a plan? You know, for when we get
    to Visaland?

LOR. *If* we get to Visaland.

ISLA. Yeah.

LOR. I dunno. Just to survive, whatever that looks like.

ISLA. Yeah but – I mean together though, right?

LOR. Yeah.

ISLA. Yeah?

HOPE. *Yeah*.

> *Beat*.

> Yeah.

> *Beat*.

> *A whistle*.

ISLA. That's the smuggler there I think.

LOR. Yeah that's him.

ISLA. Right.

> ISLA *and* LOR *stand up and go to leave*.

HOPE. Wait, um – *Lor*? Can we have a word, actually? Before we…

LOR (*nods. To* ISLA). We'll meet you down there.

> ISLA *leaves*.

> So?

> *Beat*.

> What is it?

HOPE. I uh – don't think I'm coming.

LOR. What?

HOPE. I think I'm gonna stay.

LOR. Are you joking?

HOPE. No.

LOR. They'll kill you, Hope.

HOPE. I know but –

LOR. They will kill you.

HOPE. I *know* but I can't leave him. I can't leave Mitch, not again – not without seeing him.

LOR. Right but you're happy to leave *me*? *Again?*

HOPE (*shrugs*).

Beat.

LOR. Fine.

She takes out an old-looking mobile phone.

Here then.

Beat.

HOPE. What's this?

LOR. His number.

HOPE. *What?* But how did you get it?

LOR. I *always* had it.

HOPE. So the stuff about him running away –

LOR. Yeah that was true but later he got back in touch. I just
    didn't trust you not to hurt him again. But now, if you're
    staying, I figured I may as well give it to you and –

HOPE *embraces* LOR *tightly*.

LOR *doesn't really embrace her back*.

Pause.

Are you gonna take it then or –

HOPE. Oh yeah.

Embrace ends.

HOPE *copies the number into her phone then passes* LOR*'s
    phone back*.

Thank you.

LOR (*nods*).

HOPE. Do you think he'll want to see me?

LOR. I dunno.

HOPE. But like would *you*? You know, if it were you – if you
    were Mitch and I called after all these years, would *you* want
    to meet me?

LOR. Probably not, no.

HOPE. Oh.

LOR. But it's worth trying, isn't it? It's all you *can* do.

Pause.

Anyway. I should really –

Two whistles.

Yep.

HOPE. Well, um – goodbye, I guess.

LOR. Bye, Hope.

HOPE. I'll see you in twenty-four years, maybe.

LOR. Maybe.

LOR *starts to leave.*

Beat.

HOPE. Oh and uh – say goodbye to Isla for me, will you?

LOR*'s gone.*

Pause.

HOPE *stares at her phone, still wearing the lifejacket.*

She eventually makes a phone call.

Blackout.

*

A McDonald's.

HOPE *is sitting at a table alone.*

On the table are two untouched Happy Meals.

CUSTOMER *approaches.*

CUSTOMER. You using this chair?

HOPE. What?

CUSTOMER. Oh – um, I was just wondering if I could take this chair, or –

HOPE. Oh no I'm waiting for someone. I mean he's late but he did say to meet him here, so. *Sorry.*

CUSTOMER *nods and leaves.*

Long pause.

'We'll Meet Again' by the Ink Spots plays.

Plays for at least ten seconds.

Blackout.

A Nick Hern Book

Hope has a Happy Meal first published in Great Britain in 2023 as a paperback original by Nick Hern Books Limited, The Glasshouse, 49a Goldhawk Road, London W12 8QP, in association with the Royal Court Theatre, London

Hope has a Happy Meal copyright © 2023 Tom Fowler

Tom Fowler has asserted his right to be identified as the author of this work

Cover image: Helen Murray / ArenaPAL

Designed and typeset by Nick Hern Books, London
Printed in Great Britain by Mimeo Ltd, Huntingdon, Cambridgeshire PE29 6XX

A CIP catalogue record for this book is available from the British Library

ISBN 978 1 83904 234 8

www.nickhernbooks.co.uk/environmental-policy

www.nickhernbooks.co.uk

facebook.com/nickhernbooks

twitter.com/nickhernbooks